# HILLARY RODHAM CLINTON

# HILLARY RODHAM CLINTON

Richard Kozar

CHELSEA HOUSE PUBLISHERS
PHILADELPHIA

**Chelsea House Publishers**
EDITOR-IN-CHIEF Stephen Reginald
MANAGING EDITOR James D. Gallagher
PRODUCTION MANAGER Pam Loos
ART DIRECTOR Sara Davis
PHOTO EDITOR Judy Hasday
SENIOR PRODUCTION EDITOR Lisa Chippendale

Staff for **Hillary Clinton**
SENIOR EDITOR Jim Gallagher
EDITORIAL ASSISTANT Anne Hill
PICTURE RESEARCHER Sandy Jones
ASSOCIATE ART DIRECTOR Takeshi Takahashi
DESIGNER Keith Trego
COVER ILLUSTRATION Bob Commander

1 3 5 7 9 8 6 4 2

**Library of Congress Cataloging-in-Publication Data**

Kozar, Richard.
Hillary Rodham Clinton / Richard Kozar.
p. cm. —(Women of Achievement)
Includes bibliographical references and index.
Summary: Examines the childhood, family life, and social and
 political activities of this powerful and important First Lady.

ISBN 0-7910-4712-1 (hc). — ISBN 0-7910-4713-X (pbk).

1. Clinton, Hillary Rodham—Juvenile literature. 2. Presidents' spouses—
United States—Biography—Juvenile literature. [1. Clinton, Hillary Rodham.
2. First ladies. 3. Women—Biography.] I. Title. II. Series.
E887.C55K69 1998
973.929'092—dc21
[B]                                                             97-45702
                                                                  CIP
                                                                   AC

# CONTENTS

# WOMEN of ACHIEVEMENT

**Abigail Adams**
WOMEN'S RIGHTS ADVOCATE

**Jane Addams**
SOCIAL WORKER

**Madeleine Albright**
POLITICIAN

**Louisa May Alcott**
AUTHOR

**Marian Anderson**
SINGER

**Susan B. Anthony**
WOMAN SUFFRAGIST

**Ethel Barrymore**
ACTRESS

**Clara Barton**
AMERICAN RED CROSS FOUNDER

**Elizabeth Blackwell**
PHYSICIAN

**Pearl Buck**
AUTHOR

**Margaret Bourke-White**
PHOTOGRAPHER

**Rachel Carson**
BIOLOGIST AND AUTHOR

**Mary Cassatt**
ARTIST

**Hillary Rodham Clinton**
FIRST LADY/ATTORNEY

**Emily Dickinson**
POET

**Isadora Duncan**
DANCER

**Amelia Earhart**
AVIATOR

**Betty Friedan**
FEMINIST

**Althea Gibson**
TENNIS CHAMPION

**Helen Hayes**
ACTRESS

**Katharine Hepburn**
ACTRESS

**Anne Hutchinson**
RELIGIOUS LEADER

**Mahalia Jackson**
GOSPEL SINGER

**Helen Keller**
HUMANITARIAN

**Jeane Kirkpatrick**
DIPLOMAT

**Barbara McClintock**
BIOLOGIST

**Margaret Mead**
ANTHROPOLOGIST

**Edna St. Vincent Millay**
POET

**Agnes de Mille**
CHOREOGRAPHER

**Julia Morgan**
ARCHITECT

**Grandma Moses**
PAINTER

**Georgia O'Keeffe**
PAINTER

**Sandra Day O'Connor**
SUPREME COURT JUSTICE

**Rosie O'Donnell**
ENTERTAINER/COMEDIENNE

**Eleanor Roosevelt**
DIPLOMAT AND HUMANITARIAN

**Wilma Rudolph**
CHAMPION ATHLETE

**Diana, Princess of Wales**
HUMANITARIAN

**Gloria Steinem**
FEMINIST

**Harriet Beecher Stowe**
AUTHOR AND ABOLITIONIST

**Elizabeth Taylor**
ACTRESS/ACTIVIST

**Barbara Walters**
JOURNALIST

**Edith Wharton**
AUTHOR

**Phyllis Wheatley**
POET

**Babe Didrikson Zaharias**
CHAMPION ATHLETE

# "REMEMBER THE LADIES"

## MATINA S. HORNER

"Remember the Ladies." That is what Abigail Adams wrote to her husband John, then a delegate to the Continental Congress, as the Founding Fathers met in Philadelphia to form a new nation in March of 1776. "Be more generous and favorable to them than your ancestors. Do not put such limited power in the hands of the Husbands. If particular care and attention is not paid to the Ladies," Abigail Adams warned, "we are determined to foment a Rebellion, and will not hold ourselves bound by any Laws in which we have no voice, or Representation."

The words of Abigail Adams, one of the earliest American advocates of women's rights, were prophetic. Because when we have not "remembered the ladies," they have, by their words and deeds, reminded us so forcefully of the omission that we cannot fail to remember them. For the history of American women is as interesting and varied as the history of our nation as a whole. American women have played an integral part in founding, settling, and building our country. Some we remember as remarkable women who—against great odds—achieved distinction in the public arena: Anne Hutchinson, who in the 17th century became a charismatic religious leader; Phillis Wheatley, an 18th-century black slave who became a poet; Susan B. Anthony, whose name is synonymous with the 19th-century women's rights movement, and who led the struggle to enfranchise women; and in the 20th century, Amelia Earhart, the first woman to cross the Atlantic Ocean by air.

These extraordinary women certainly merit our admiration, but other women, "common women," many of them all but forgotten, should also be recognized for their contributions to American thought and culture. Women have been community builders; they have founded schools and formed voluntary associations to help those in need; they have assumed the major responsibility for rearing children, passing on from one generation to the next the values that keep a culture alive. These and innumerable other contributions, once ignored, are now being recognized by scholars, students, and the public. It is exciting and gratifying that a part of our history that was hardly acknowledged a few generations ago is now being studied and brought to light.

In recent decades, the field of women's history has grown from obscurity to a politically controversial splinter movement to academic respectability, in many cases mainstreamed into such traditional disciplines as history, economics, and psychology. Scholars of women, both female and male, have organized research centers at such prestigious institutions as Wellesley College, Stanford University, and the University of California. Other notable centers for women's studies are the Center for the American Woman and Politics at the Eagleton Institute of Politics at Rutgers University; the Henry A. Murray Research Center for the Study of Lives, at Radcliffe College; and the Women's Research and Education Institute, the research arm of the Congressional Caucus on Women's Issues. Other scholars and public figures have established archives and libraries, such as the Schlesinger Library on the History of Women in America, at Radcliffe College, and the Sophia Smith Collection, at Smith College, to collect and preserve the written and tangible legacies of women.

From the initial donation of the Women's Rights Collection in 1943, the Schlesinger Library grew to encompass vast collections documenting the manifold accomplishments of American women. Simultaneously, the women's movement in general and the academic discipline of women's studies in particular also began with a narrow definition and gradually expanded their mandate. Early causes, such as woman suffrage and social reform, abolition, and organized labor were joined by newer concerns, such as the history of women in business and the professions and in politics and government; the study of the family; and social issues such as health policy and education.

Women, as historian Arthur M. Schlesinger, jr., once pointed out, "have constituted the most spectacular casualty of traditional history. They have made up at least half the human race, but you could never tell that by looking at the books historians write." The new breed of historians is remedying that omission. They have written books about immigrant women and about working-class women who struggled for survival in cities and about black women who met the challenges of life in rural areas. They are telling the stories of women who, despite the barriers of tradition and economics, became lawyers and doctors and public figures.

The women's studies movement has also led scholars to question traditional interpretations of their respective disciplines. For example, the study of war has traditionally been an exercise in military and political analysis, an examination of strategies planned and executed by men. But scholars of women's history have pointed out that wars have also been periods of tremendous change and even opportunity for women, because the very absence of men on the home front enabled them to expand their educational, economic, and professional activities and to assume leadership in their homes.

The early scholars of women's history showed a unique brand of courage in choosing to investigate new subjects and take new approaches to old ones. Often, like their subjects, they endured criticism and even ostracism by their academic colleagues. But their efforts have unquestionably been worthwhile, because with the publication of each new study and book another piece of the historical patchwork is sewn into place, revealing an increasingly comprehensive picture of the role of women in our rich and varied history.

Such books on groups of women are essential, but books that focus on the lives of individuals are equally indispensable. Biographies can be inspirational, offering their readers the example of people with vision who have looked outside themselves for their goals and have often struggled against great obstacles to achieve them. Marian Anderson, for instance, had to overcome racial bigotry in order to perfect her art and perform as a concert singer. Isadora Duncan defied the rules of classical dance to find true artistic freedom. Jane Addams had to break down society's notions of the proper role for women in order to create new social situations, notably the settlement house. All of these women had to come to terms both with themselves and with the world in which they lived. Only then could they move ahead as pioneers in their chosen callings.

Biography can inspire not only by adulation but also by realism. It helps us to see not only the qualities in others that we hope to emulate, but also, perhaps, the weaknesses that made them "human." By helping us identify with the subject on a more personal level they help us feel that we, too, can achieve such goals. We read about Eleanor Roosevelt, for instance, who occupied a unique and seemingly enviable position as the wife of the president. Yet we can sympathize with her inner dilemma; an inherently shy woman, she had to force herself to live a most public life in order to use her position to benefit others. We may not be able to imagine ourselves having the immense poetic talent of Emily Dickinson, but from her story we can understand the challenges faced by a creative woman who was expected to fulfill many family responsibilities. And though few of us will ever reach the level of athletic accomplishment displayed by Wilma Rudolph or Babe Zaharias, we can still appreciate their spirit, their overwhelming will to excel.

A biography is a multifaceted lens. It is first of all a magnification, the intimate examination of one particular life. But at the same time, it is a wide-angle lens, informing us about the world in which the subject lived. We come away from reading about one life knowing more about the social, political, and economic fabric of the time. It is for this reason, perhaps, that the great New England essayist Ralph Waldo Emerson wrote in 1841, "There is properly no history: only biography." And it is also why biography, and particularly women's biography, will continue to fascinate writers and readers alike.

*As first lady, Hillary Rodham Clinton is unlike any of her predecessors. She has been involved in important political initiatives, such as health-care reform and child care, and has advocated education improvements and women's rights.*

# 1

# FIRST LADY
# LIKE NO OTHER

Hillary Rodham Clinton has done more to redefine the image of America's first lady than any of her predecessors, including one of her role models, Eleanor Roosevelt, who was also an active and forceful partner in her husband's presidency. Mrs. Clinton's first job after moving into the White House in 1993 was to oversee a select committee charged with national health-care reform. While the effort, which faced stiff opposition from within the health-care industry, eventually failed, it signaled to the entire country that this first lady would not content herself with programs like outdoor beautification or redecorating the White House.

Several first ladies have had tremendous influence on their husbands and national policy, but until Bill Clinton's presidency, none has had as visible—nor as powerful—a role as Hillary Rodham Clinton. Although the first lady's office has been traditionally located in the ceremonial East Wing of the White House, hers is located in the West Wing, not far from the president's Oval Office, where decisions affecting the nation and the world are reached.

Mrs. Clinton's broadened role certainly reflects her skills as an accomplished attorney and an organizer. However, to a consider-

*During her career, Hillary has always been involved in children's issues. This photo was taken when Hillary was speaking at a conference on child welfare and development that was held in Kansas City in 1997.*

able degree, her life also mirrors the slow but sure rise of influential women in America. Unlike Mrs. Roosevelt, Hillary Rodham Clinton assumed the once-symbolic post of first lady at a point in history when almost 60 percent of American women work, either by necessity or choice. In addition, many women of her generation have earned college- and graduate-level degrees, unlike their counterparts half a century ago.

The feminist movement, seeking social and economic equality for women in a male-dominated nation, has come a long way since 1920, when Congress finally passed the 19th Amendment to the Constitution granting women the legal right to vote. The strides were especially long in the early 1970s, when women like Hillary were graduating from college and putting their views into practice.

For example, she felt compelled to go by her maiden name, Rodham, even after marrying Bill Clinton in 1975. The decision reflected not just a lifelong vow to stake out a professional identity for herself, but growing feminist empowerment. At the time, she was perfectly capable of earning her own living and could have had her pick of jobs in some of the nation's most prestigious metropolitan law firms. In fact, for the next several years Arkansas's first lady would earn several times more money as a lawyer and corporate board member than her politician husband.

Unfortunately, the public's sentiments on the changing roles of women—particularly prominent, visible ones—don't always march in step with the times, a fact made crystal clear to Hillary Rodham after her husband had been elected attorney general and then governor of Arkansas. Her decision to retain her maiden name, along with her refusal to dress fashionably and wear makeup, were as much to blame for Bill Clinton's bitter reelection defeat in his second race for governor as any of his administration's shortcomings, voters said after the campaign.

In a concession two years later to the legions of Arkansas voters who had never approved of her "hifalutin' Yankee ways," she swallowed her pride and publicly stated she would henceforth go by Hillary Rodham Clinton. After she made the announcement, Bill Clinton ran again and this time won a second term as governor. It wouldn't be the last time Arkansas's first

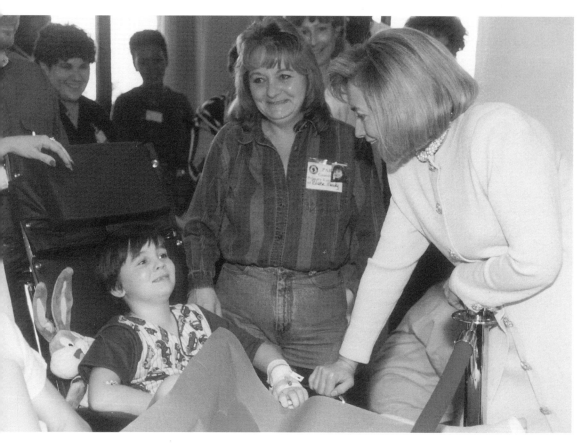

*Hillary meets a young patient in the Natal Intensive Care Unit (NICU) that she helped to create at Arkansas Children's Hospital.*

lady compromised for the sake of her husband's bright political future.

However, the flap over her insistence on using her maiden name would be a relatively minor storm compared to the numerous public and private tempests that have beset Hillary and Bill Clinton ever since their unique partnership began in Arkansas. An unprecedented number of investigations and inquiries into events that took place decades ago in Arkansas, such as the Whitewater land deal, and more recent politial intrigues in the White House, have still not subsided. Certainly, partisan witch-hunts against this Democratic couple explain a degree of the preoccupation with their ethics, but several longtime Clinton associates have already gone to jail for their roles in the Arkansas dealings and pointed accusing fingers at the Clintons themselves.

Thus, the final years of the 20th century will determine whether Hillary Rodham Clinton's legacy will ultimately be as an acclaimed advocate for children's and women's rights and as a proponent of national health-care reform, or for her role in headline-making controversies.

*Hillary Rodham in sixth grade at Eugene Field Elementary School. Even at a young age, Hillary was very mature, her mother later recalled.*

2

# GROWING UP

Hillary Rodham was among the first wave of children who make up a generation that's been dubbed the "baby boomers," those born in the years following the end of World War II. She made her entrance—all eight pounds, five ounces of her—on October 26, 1947, the only daughter of three children born to Hugh and Dorothy Rodham.

Hillary came into the world at a good time for a 20th-century infant, during the period of economic growth in the United States that followed the Second World War. The country was in transition between the thrifty generation that had suffered through the Great Depression and one that would reap the benefits of the coming decade's prosperity.

The onset of peace in 1945 between the United States and wartime enemies Germany and Japan had triggered an explosion not just in the birth rate but in American industrial production as well. Factories that had previously been operating all-out to support the war effort were now just as busy making steel for the nation's expanding highway system and for the cars that consumers purchased to drive on these highways.

Both businesses and workers enjoyed the surge in prosperity. For the most part, the workforce of the 1950s was made up of men who were the sole providers for their families. Wives and mothers, many of whom had labored in the factories only years earlier while their fathers, brothers, or sweethearts fought overseas, were now expected to run a household instead.

Although Hillary's mother, Dorothy Howell, stayed at home to raise her daughter and two sons, she had the temperament and yearning to spread her wings and become an independent career woman. The daughter of blue-collar, working parents in South Chicago—her mother could barely read and write—Dorothy would eventually blossom when the family moved to Los Angeles. There she would excel academically and athletically in high school, only to return to Chicago following graduation, where she met a young curtain salesman named Hugh Rodham.

Seven years older than Dorothy, Hugh had been raised by working-class parents in the coal-mining town of Scranton, Pennsylvania. By most accounts, his upbringing was strict and severe, reflecting his English and Methodist ancestry.

A fine athlete, Hugh faced and overcame incredible adversity early in his life; his feet and legs were crushed in an accident and would have been amputated if not for the intervention of his defiant mother, who forbade doctors from performing the surgery. Remarkably, he recovered, and after much hard work he became a high school football star, winning a scholarship to attend Penn State University in Pennsylvania, where he majored in physical education. After college, he returned to Scranton and went to work in the same lace factory that had employed his father.

Eventually, Hugh Rodham moved to Chicago, landed a job as a salesman in the fabric business, and met Dorothy. After a five-year courtship, he and Dorothy married in 1942, less than a year after the Japanese

launched their surprise attack on Pearl Harbor and drew America into World War II.

Hugh put his college training to work by joining the U.S. Navy, supervising young recruits in conditioning and self-defense at the Great Lakes Naval Base north of Chicago. He and other trainers around the country in similar positions were expected to turn green young men—many barely out of high school—into tough soldiers to wage the nation's war abroad.

By several accounts, Hugh Rodham raised his children, including his daughter, as if they, too, were flabby recruits and he their stern drill sergeant.

The first lady's portrayal of her father is flattering. Her family "was like *Father Knows Best,*" she has said,

*After Hillary was born, Hugh and Dorothy Rodham moved the family out of Chicago to this home in Park Ridge, an affluent suburb.*

referring to a 1950s television sitcom that featured a wise, good-natured father figure rearing three youngsters with the help of his supportive, neatly dressed wife.

However, Hillary's brother, Hugh Jr., later confirmed that the Rodhams' father employed a confrontational approach, a technique that worked in boot camp but could be unsettling on the home front. In addition, Hugh Rodham could be as stingy as a miser with praise. In a telling remark following Hillary's latest in a series of straight-A report cards in junior high, Hugh said, "Well, Hillary, that must be an easy school you go to." According to Hugh Jr., after Hillary managed similar high marks in college courses, their father said, "It must be a pretty small college."

But rather than break her considerable spirit, her father's high expectations actually drove her to succeed even more, Hillary says in retrospect. And in her estimation, her brothers bore the brunt of their father's challenging demeanor. Once, after her younger brother Tony guided his high school football team to a shutout victory in a championship game in which he completed 10 of 11 passes he threw, an unimpressed Hugh said Tony should have completed the other one.

Years afterward, Dorothy would recall her husband's refusal to dole out praise or allowances as his way of avoiding spoiled children. She said, "He'd declare, 'They eat and sleep for free. We're not going to pay them for it as well!'"

Perhaps it is fortunate, then, that Hillary was described by her mother as "very mature upon birth." (Her name itself comes from a family name that Dorothy thought was exotic and unusual.) From an early age, Hillary's maturity served her well. "Boys responded well to Hillary," Dorothy recalled. "She just took charge, and they let her." The oldest of the Rodham children was trustworthy enough to babysit her two younger brothers, and at age 13 she landed her first "real" job, supervising children at a nearby park

during summer mornings.

But her maturity and confidence were also forged by the struggles all youngsters eventually face in the world beyond the comfort of their homes. Hillary recalls one particular instance in her book, *It Takes A Village*: "Once, while I was still in grade school, an older boy who was visiting in the area chased me, threw me to the ground, and kissed me until I kicked and hit him hard enough to extricate myself and scramble home."

Her mother's advice? Dorothy asked her daughter, "Do you want to be the lead actor in your life, or a minor player who simply reacts to what others think

*Hillary and her parents, Hugh and Dorothy Rodham, share a moment together during the 1992 Democratic National Convention.*

*Hillary (middle row, second from left) was interested in politics at a young age. As a senior at Maine South High School, she was a member of the student council.*

you should say or do?" According to Roger Morris, author of *Partners in Power*, Dorothy was determined that "no daughter of mine was going to have to go through the agony of being afraid to say what she had on her mind. Just because she was a girl didn't mean she should be limited."

In an interview with a French magazine, Dorothy also related how she impressed upon her daughter the importance of education. "I explained to [Hillary] very early that school was a great adventure . . . that she was going to learn great things, live new passions. I motivated her in a way that she wasn't 'resigned' to go to school. I wanted her to be excited by the idea. Maybe that's why Hillary was never afraid. Not of school. Not of anything."

And when Hillary would find herself in a jam, father Hugh had a predictable response that she says influences her to this day. "Hillary, how are you going to dig yourself out of this one?" he'd ask.

"His query always brought to mind a shovel," she wrote in her 1996 book. "That image stayed with me, and over the course of my life I have reached for mental, emotional, and spiritual shovels of various shapes and sizes—even a backhoe or two."

One of her early setbacks was discovering that her dream of becoming an astronaut was indeed only a dream. In the early 1960s, Americans were consumed by the race in space and the goal of catching up with the Russians, who had launched the first Sputnik rocket into orbit. Hillary sent a letter to the National Aeronautic and Space Administration (NASA) asking how to become an astronaut. She was told girls weren't accepted into the program, a response that infuriated her. Her only consolation later was that her poor eyesight probably would have kept her earthbound anyway.

As Hillary and her brothers were growing up, Hugh started his own independent drapery business. With the success of the venture, the Rodhams could eventually afford to leave the confines of their tiny apartment in downtown Chicago and move to a manicured suburb outside the city known as Park Ridge.

While the postwar years sparked a home-building rush in major metropolitan suburbs around the country, Park Ridge was far from a dusty, growing development. By 1950, it was an established, tree-lined community, populated almost entirely by white, upper-middle-class families that were staunchly Republican, a political party associated with affluence and a legendary distrust of big government.

By contrast, inner-city Chicago had a colorful history as a stronghold of Democrats, the opposing political party of 20th century America that was typically associated with government social programs like welfare and Social Security—and levying hefty taxes to pay for them.

It is ironic that Hillary Rodham, raised in the comfortable lap of Park Ridge's Republican lifestyle, would later switch alliances by embracing the Democratic Party, which her husband would eventually lead into the White House. Even more remarkable, after meeting Bill Clinton her uncompromising Republican father would become one of his biggest supporters.

As she would throughout her life, Hillary was recognized even at a young age for being serious, analytical, logical, and organized, all of which made her a natural in the world of books, academics, and achievement. After she joined the Brownies and Girl Scouts, she predictably earned a sash filled with badges and pins. In time, through the family's Methodist church, she helped help care for children of migrant farmworkers who, before suburban sprawl replaced rural Chicago farmland, camped out on the city's outskirts to pick fruits and vegetables.

Her business-minded father even went so far as to teach her to understand stock market tables, which report the daily price fluctuations in the nation's financial markets. Making money was a serious endeavor for Hugh Rodham, so much so that he played investing games with his daughter at a young age, a lesson that Hillary was destined to apply in her own life to great advantage later on.

By most measures, Dorothy Rodham was the stereotypical 1950s mother, providing meals and a nurturing environment for her family as well as teaching Sunday school, attending all school and athletic events, and driving the neighborhood kids to their destinations. Dorothy had decided early on that her daughter would have opportunities that most women

of her generation—and of Dorothy's own generation—would never have.

"My mother and father did what parents do best,"
recalled Hillary. "They dedicated their time, energy,
and money to their children and made sacrifices to give
us a better life."

*Hillary Rodham was caught in a lighthearted moment by a photographer for the Wellesley College yearbook. Wellesley was a new world for the bright, young student.*

# 3

# THE WORLD BEYOND PARK RIDGE

Hillary credits her Methodist church's youth group for exposing her to a side of America she had never seen as a young girl in the sheltered world of Park Ridge. The year was 1960. Vice president Richard Nixon was running for president against a young, charismatic Irishman from Massachusetts named John F. Kennedy, a Democrat. Hillary was 13.

At the First United Methodist Church, a new youth minister was appointed: 30-year-old Donald Jones. Conscious of the growing friction between young and old and the tumultuous conflicts the 1960s would come to symbolize, Jones was determined to introduce the impressionable youths of the church group to life beyond the confines of Park Ridge. "We were just getting out of the Eisenhower era, the Pat Boone era, the passive period, and moving into the revolutionary decade where so many things would happen," Jones said in Judith Warner's book, *Hillary Clinton, The Inside Story.* "Kennedy had just been elected, and the civil rights laws would be passed within two years. That's when I first got in touch with Hillary."

Jones took the church group teens on field trips to the worst

*Two people who helped shape Hillary's idealism were President John F. Kennedy (left) and the Rev. Martin Luther King Jr. (right). Another of Hillary's early influences was a young minister in Park Ridge's Methodist Church, Donald Jones, who introduced new experiences to Hillary and her peers in Park Ridge.*

Chicago inner-city neighborhoods, where Hillary and her peers learned what life was like for hardened kids on the streets. It was her first glimpse of the world that less fortunate people had to contend with, and the visits made her appreciate how lucky she had been.

"I don't think those kids had seen poverty before. I don't think they had interacted with kids that weren't like themselves," Jones later said. "Religion, going to church, tended to function there for most people to reinforce their rather traditional conservative values. And so when I came in and took that white middle-class youth group into the inner city of Chicago, that was quite radical."

One particular visit stands out in Hillary's mind. On April 15, 1962, Jones took his class to Chicago's

Orchestra Hall to hear Martin Luther King Jr. preach a sermon titled "Remaining Awake Through a Revolution." Afterward, Hillary met the young activist minister and shook his hand. Little did she know the southern reverend would mobilize African Americans across the United States in the coming decade, advocating racial equality through peaceful protest and resistance, only to be gunned down in the prime of his life as the turbulent '60s drew to a bloody close.

As one might expect, Donald Jones faced his own share of criticism from the church elders for the methods he employed to expand the teens' world. Still, there was no arguing about the worth of his intentions. In the early 1960s, his youth group organized food drives for the poor. In addition, he established the baby-sit-

*At Maine South High School, Hillary Rodham (bottom row, left) graduated 15th in her class of 1,000, was a member of the National Honor Society, and was a National Merit Scholarship finalist. Her classmates voted her "Most Likely to Succeed."*

ting pool Hillary would join to care for children of migrant farm workers.

During his four-year tenure at Park Ridge, Jones found Hillary a willing student, inspiring her with discussions on everything from religion to life in the changing world. "She was curious, open to what life had to bring. She was just insatiable," Jones would later say. The close bond Hillary established with Jones would evolve into an ongoing correspondence that continued even after she became first lady.

Jones went so far as to defend Hillary when a

reporter suggested the first lady hadn't had much of a social life in high school. "Boys liked her," Jones said in *Partners in Power*. "And not because she was flirtatious. She was not. She wasn't a raving beauty, but she was pretty enough. What attracted guys around her was her personality, her willingness to talk to them, at parity with them."

Hillary was definitely not a wallflower in high school. In addition to being an outstanding student, she played field hockey and volleyball, was on the debating team, had parts in school plays, and sang in variety shows (even though she was the first to admit she was tone-deaf).

One thing was certain: Hillary wasn't a slave to fashion or public opinion. She wore no makeup and cared little about the plainness of her hairstyle. As an adult, she would tell the *Washington Post*: "I saw a lot of my friends who had been really lively and smart and doing well in school beginning to worry that boys would think they were too smart, or beginning to cut back on how well they did or the courses they took, because that's not where their boyfriends were. And I can recall thinking, 'Gosh, why are they doing that?' It didn't make sense to me."

At least as a teen, dating held little attraction for her, according to classmates. However, that didn't prevent her from seeking out the company of intelligent boys, to whom she was more than willing to devote time.

Her first brush with national politics came during her senior year, when she actively campaigned for conservative presidential candidate Barry Goldwater, going so far as to orchestrate a political convention in the gym emulating the national Republican Party's event.

She would graduate 15th out of 1,000 students in the class of '65 and be a National Merit Scholarship finalist, a student council leader, and a member of the National Honor Society. Moreover, she was voted the girl "Most Likely to Succeed."

*Hillary decided to attend Wellesley College, an elite school for women only, even though it was located 1,000 miles from her home and family. She joined several organizations, including Wellesley's Young Republican Club. This picture was taken in February 1968 when Hillary (center), a junior, was running for president of the student government. She won, defeating classmates Nonna Noto (left) and Francille Rusan (right).*

Like her fellow classmates, she had goals beyond high school, including one she wrote down for posterity in the Maine South High paper: "To marry a senator and settle down in Georgetown."

There was never a question that Hillary would go on to college, thanks to the financial security her father's business provided. The only question was where.

Unlike most of her classmates, who preferred to attend college closer to home, she was intrigued by Radcliffe, Smith, and Wellesley, elite colleges located near Boston, Massachusetts. One of her teachers her senior year had attended Smith; another had gone to nearby Wellesley College. They urged her to consider these "Seven Sisters" schools, so named because they were among seven prestigious colleges that admitted only women. Ultimately, Hillary settled on Wellesley. It had a reputation for attracting young women from the most well-to-do families on the East Coast and bore a tuition to reflect its status. In the mid-1960s, Wellesley was more expensive to attend than several of the equally renowned, predominantly male Ivy League schools in the East.

Although she was happy that her daughter was making her way into a larger world, Dorothy Rodham was nonetheless apprehensive about thrusting Hillary into an unfamiliar setting over 1,000 miles from home. She feared her daughter had led too sheltered a life for the challenges college and the '60s pop culture would impose.

Dorothy's concern was unfounded, however. After school began, Hillary adjusted quickly to campus life, even joining Wellesley's Young Republican organization (which she would later lead as president) and the student senate, where she learned to lobby for campus improvements. Her major at Wellesley was political science.

A former college boyfriend during her years at Wellesley said the future first lady was most memorable for her eagerness to engage in conversation about the issues of the day. "She would rather sit around and talk about current events or politics or ideas than go bicycle riding or to a football game," he told author Roger Morris.

In addition, Hillary was full of political zeal, said her boyfriend, even though at the time she wasn't exactly sure how to target her enthusiasm. "From the first time I met her, I remember being struck by her real interest in government from the point of view of someone who wanted to be involved and have an impact, but [she] didn't know exactly how," he said. "She didn't have fixed ambitions in terms of knowing that she wanted to be elected to some office, and she certainly didn't give any indication that she was looking to attach herself to a politician—and I'm sure probably would have been offended by that concept if someone had raised it at the time."

And, in a sign of her career to come, Hillary developed a reputation for mediating disagreements on campus, a skill that would serve her well in the legal profession.

At the same time, her world continued to expand beyond the narrow confines of the conservative Republican upbringing that had defined her youth. By volunteering to teach young African-American children living in some of the worst sections of Boston how to read, Hillary was reminded yet again how vast the gap was separating those who have from those who have not.

Children and the problems they faced had always fascinated her, which could explain the excellent grades she earned in child psychology, one of her concentrations at Wellesley. This same concern for children's well-being would remain a constant throughout her career and eventually account for some of her most notable accomplishments.

Although Wellesley wasn't disrupted by the daily protests over the Vietnam War besieging college campuses across America, students there could hardly ignore the most violent events that scarred the 1960s. On April 4, 1968, Hillary was horrified by news of the assassination of Martin Luther King Jr., the same man whose immortal "I Have A Dream" speech had echoed through Washington, D.C., five years earlier.

While news of the murder in Memphis, Tennessee, ignited rioting across the United States, Hillary and several classmates chose to join a peaceful march through downtown Boston, wearing black armbands as a symbol of mourning.

That same year, another of America's shining lights would be extinguished. Robert F. Kennedy, who had just won the California Democratic presidential primary and who was the hope of a new generation, was gunned down in a hotel lobby.

Meanwhile, the United States' involvement in Vietnam continued to escalate, despite the pledge of newly elected President Richard Nixon to bring the war to an end. With her time at Wellesley drawing to a close, Hillary was still years away from her own involvement in events that would ultimately bring down this Repub-

lican president in disgrace.

In 1969, Hillary became the first student ever chosen to give the commencement speech at Wellesley; she stunned the gathered faculty, students, and several prominent observers by launching a half-extemporaneous, half-rehearsed protest of the previous speaker, Senator Edward Brooke, a liberal Republican from Massachusetts. Hillary had been expected to reflect "the consensus of the graduating class . . . and not embarrass the college," biographer Judith Warner wrote. Instead, feeling Brooke had delivered a canned speech that all but ignored America's turmoil over the last four years, Hillary pounced on his remarks. "I find myself in a familiar position, that of reacting, something that our

*Hillary Rodham (second from left) shares smiles with Wellesley College trustee chairman John Quarles, college president Ruth Adams, and commencement speaker Massachusetts Senator Edward Brooke before the May 1969 graduation ceremony. Hillary surprised the crowd by delivering an extemporaneous indictment of the senator's speech.*

generation has been doing for quite a while now . . . I find myself reacting just briefly to some of the things that Senator Brooke said," she began.

One of her favorite professors, who thought Hillary might someday sit on the Supreme Court, observed, "She gave it to him, no ifs, ands, or buts about it." *Life* magazine, the publication credited for documenting the most poignant and tragic events of 20th century American life, carried an excerpt from the address and Hillary's picture the same year. Compared to speeches by her peers at more radical campuses across the nation, however, her address was fairly sedate.

Following graduation, in typical antiestablishment fashion, Hillary decided to see the country rather than return to her comfortable life back in Park Ridge. She headed for Alaska, even hitchhiking part of the way. There she landed a job in a salmon cannery, only to be fired soon afterward for pointing out to her employer that the fish being canned weren't fit for human consumption.

Her prior four years had been some of the most challenging in her life, her mother observed years later. "People gave her a hard time because she wanted to be the best," Dorothy Rodham said in an interview. "I think that those years were those of her greatest challenge. She was a young woman and was the equal of men. At that time that wasn't yet accepted."

Nonetheless, Hillary had decided to pursue a traditionally male career—law—and had narrowed her choices to the prestigious law schools at Harvard and Yale. A stuffy Harvard professor helped make up her mind, she later told the *Arkansas Gazette*. "I met a very distinguished, older law professor, and my friend who attended Harvard Law School said, 'Professor So-and-so, this is my friend. She's trying to decide whether to come here next year or attend our closest competitor.'

"This tall, rather imposing professor, sort of like a character from *The Paper Chase*, looked down at me

and said, 'Well, first of all, we don't have any close com-
petitors. Second, we don't need any more women.'
That's what made my decision. I was leaning toward
Yale anyway, but that fellow's comments iced the cake."

Hillary's favorite Wellesley professor, Alan Schechter,
wrote a glowing letter of recommendation to Yale.
"Hillary Rodham is by far the most outstanding young
woman I have taught in the seven years I have been on
the Wellesley College faculty," Schechter wrote. "I have
high hopes of Hillary and for her future. She has the
intellectual ability, personality, and character to make a
remarkable contribution to American society."

While at Yale, Hillary would delve even deeper into
issues affecting children, particularly what she felt were
their woefully inadequate rights under the law. Most
important, Hillary would finally meet a man who could
win her heart as well as her brain, a man with whom she
was destined to form a partnership that would lead
them to the White House.

*Wearing a gown for the 1985 Arkansas Gubernatorial Inauguration, Hillary Rodham Clinton waits for her husband, William Jefferson Clinton, whom she met at Yale University when both were students there in the early 1970s.*

4

# YALE AND BILL CLINTON

During the summer of 1970, following her first year in law school, Hillary Rodham began working for Marian Wright Edelman, a Yale Law School alumna and longtime civil rights lawyer who had founded the Washington Research Project. Edelman was the first African-American woman to pass the bar exam in Mississippi. After hearing Edelman speak at Yale, Hillary learned that she could work for the project as long as she could find the grant money to pay her salary. Tapping a program geared for students like herself at Yale, she was granted a stipend and went to Washington, D.C., where she worked with Senator Walter Mondale. His subcommittee was studying the lives of migrant farm workers and the deplorable conditions in which they lived.

Hillary also worked in the Yale Child Studies Center and volunteered to work with doctors studying cases of child abuse at New Haven Hospital. Her graduate studies included conducting research for law professor Joseph Goldstein, who edited a volume titled *Beyond the Best Interests of the Child*. The book was reprinted in Japanese, French, Swedish, and Danish. Hillary also contributed to the publication of Kenneth Keniston's *All Our Children*, which

*As a 1963 delegate to Boys' Nation, a national conference in Washington, D.C., Bill Clinton had an opportunity to meet President John F. Kennedy. Later, Clinton said that when he shook hands with the president, he knew he wanted to become a politician.*

explored such issues as parents purposely keeping children out of school for religious reasons and denial of medical care to youngsters based on their parents' religious beliefs.

In her final year at law school, Hillary was named editor of the *Yale Review of Law and Social Action*, an alternative legal journal dedicated, according to its editors, "to the development of new forms of journalism which combine scholarship of the highest standard with reflections and recommendations based on experience and practice."

In a speech to Yale's 1992 graduating class, Hillary looked back on her years in law school. "There was a great amount of ferment and confusion about what was and wasn't the proper role of law school education. We would have great arguments about whether we were selling out because we were getting a law degree, whether in fact we should be doing something else, not often defined clearly but certainly passionately argued," she said. "That we should somehow be 'out there,' where 'there' was, trying to help solve the problems that took up so much of our time in argument and discussion . . . . Those were difficult and turbulent times."

It was during her second year, however, that one of the most momentous events in her life occurred—striking up an acquaintance with one William Jefferson Clinton, a gregarious, well-liked young man from Arkansas who never left any doubt about his political ambitions before, during, or after his stint at Yale.

During a television talk show decades later, Hillary described how she and her future husband met: "The first thing I ever knew about him, and this is the truth, was when I was walking through the student lounge at Yale to get a Coke between classes. I heard this voice say, 'And not only that, we grow the biggest watermelons in the world.'"

Hillary remembers saying to a friend, "Who *is that?*"

"That's Bill Clinton," was the reply. "He's from Arkansas. That's all he ever talks about."

Hillary continued: "Finally one day, he was standing outside the law school library. And I was in, trying to study, but I was kind of keeping my eye on him. And he kept kind of looking at me, and finally, I went up to him, and I said, 'You know, if we're going to keep looking at each other, we ought to at least know each other's name.'"

Bill Clinton was unlike any man Hillary had ever met, in ways that contrasted with her own personality. He was sparkling, effervescent, persuasive, and quick-thinking; she, in turn, has been described by observers as logical, analytical, calculating, and methodical.

Moreover, he was an unabashed "good ole boy" from Arkansas, one of the most impoverished states in

*Together, Bill and Hillary Clinton have forged a partnership that has taken them to the White House.*

the country, and a Southern Baptist raised by a single mother who was loving but also hard-pressed to provide a stable home life. Unlike Hillary Rodham, Clinton grew up in a predominantly black neighborhood of a town called Hope. His first home did not have indoor plumbing, and his mother, Virginia, had to leave him with his grandparents after his real father, William Jefferson Blythe, died in an auto accident, leaving her to support their son. She left the young boy in her parents' care while she pursued nurse anesthetist training in New Orleans, Louisiana.

When Bill was four, his mother married Roger Clinton, a hopeless alcoholic who would periodically beat and verbally abuse his wife and stepson until Bill had grown into a six-foot, 200-pound young man and put a stop to the terror. Virginia Clinton recalled later that, as Roger was beating her, Bill broke down the bedroom door, picked up his drunk stepfather, and said, "Hear me—Never . . . ever . . . touch my mother again."

Virginia eventually had a second son, Roger Clinton, who would later in life fall into a pattern of cocaine abuse eerily reminiscent of his father's affliction. His habit ultimately landed him in prison.

Without a doubt Hillary Rodham and Bill Clinton were from different worlds. That the two young Yale law students should fall in love practically at first sight is remarkable considering that about the only things they had in common were intelligence and ambition.

Because the first couple is a team in every sense of the word, one cannot look at the person Hillary has become without also looking at the man whose career she put before hers time and again, although doing so went against her ideals. Indeed, at critical points in her life, Hillary chose to follow her husband's path rather than one she could have charted on her own.

But people who have known Bill Clinton over the years have little trouble understanding why he could spark that kind of devotion. By most measures, he has a remarkable gift for inspiring those around him and for captivating their attention with his natural warmth, charisma, and intense desire to please. "Bill exhibited all the signs of someone who was on the way to somewhere else [and] in a hurry to get there," said a friend. "If he had not been so totally amiable, genuinely kind, open, and friendly, he would have been heartily disliked by one and all, but he had absolutely no pretense about him, and that, of course, made him irresistible."

His critics would argue that his beguiling personality disguises a darker side, one that is willing to say and do whatever is necessary to achieve a goal. Yet even his detractors admit Bill Clinton has a way with people, a talent for convincing them of the rightness of what he's saying, whether in person or viewed by millions of people on television. Former president Ronald Reagan was known as the "Great Communicator," and President Bill Clinton can be considered the heir to this title.

But a man who aspires to the highest office in the land must be able to persuade voters of his worth, to convince them he is the candidate they should elect over all challengers. That, by most yardsticks, is the definition of a politician. And if nothing else, Clinton is the consummate politician, a career choice he never wavered from or felt obliged to apologize for.

In high school, Clinton, like his future wife, excelled in math and science and also acted, winning the starring role in the school play. Clinton also loved music, and at one time actually considered becoming a professional musician. He was selected the first chair tenor saxophone player in the Arkansas All-State First Band.

But it was government that caught his fancy, due in large part to the 1963 trip he made as a delegate to Boys' Nation in Washington, D.C. There, he met two people who would have a powerful influence on his life: Arkansas Democratic Senator J. William Fulbright, the powerful chairman of the Senate Foreign Relations Committee, and President John F. Kennedy. Clinton says that when as a teenager he shook hands with the president, he knew he wanted to be a politician.

"I decided to be a Democrat, starting in the presidential election of 1960, when John Kennedy excited me with a promise to get the country moving again," Bill Clinton said years later. "I think he gave people the sense that they could make a difference. And he did it without ever promising that all the problems would be solved—just that tomorrow would be better than today. He convinced me that he and Lyndon Johnson wanted to do something about civil rights problems, particularly in the South, my own region."

In another interview, quoted in Norman King's book *Hillary: Her True Story*, Clinton said, "By the time I was 17, I knew I wanted to be what I'm doing now [being a politician] . . . and I knew that if I was in school in Washington, I would have many opportunities to learn a lot about foreign affairs, domestic politics, and economics.

"I just started asking people, including staff members of our congressional delegation, what was the most appropriate place," Clinton continued. "The consensus was that the School of Foreign Service at Georgetown was the most appropriate and the most academically respected and rigorous."

While at Georgetown University in Washington, D.C., a conservative Jesuit school, he applied for and was awarded a Rhodes scholarship, a coveted opportunity to study at Oxford University in England. He spent two years there, from 1968 to 1970.

As Clinton studied in England, the war continued to rage in Vietnam. Understandably, many young American men like him preferred not to enlist or be drafted into the army to fight in a protested conflict where tens of thousands of soldiers had already lost their lives. For some, college provided a temporary haven to escape the draft, as did enrollment in branches of the service where active duty was unlikely, such as the U.S.

Coast Guard. And for a relative few, fleeing to Canada or other countries was the only means of dodging a tour in Vietnam.

Bill Clinton was among those college students who managed to avoid the draft while at Oxford; critics would say years later it was because he did everything in his power to do so. In any event, his good fortune would earn him the nickname "Slick Willie" when his patriotism was questioned in future political campaigns.

Clinton left Oxford in 1970 to accept a scholarship at Yale, where he thought his career would be better served. Those who knew him there remembered him as someone eager to make his mark on the world. Not surprisingly, acquaintances of Hillary Rodham paint a similar picture of her during those same years.

*In a sign of things to come, Arkansas Governor Bill Clinton and Hillary Rodham enter the White House to attend a dinner honoring the governors of all 50 states in February 1979. Fourteen years later, Bill would be elected president of the United States.*

# 5

# BUILDING A CAREER AND A FAMILY

B y Hillary's third year at Yale, she and Bill had grown so close
that they began sharing an apartment. Although unmarried
couples living together might have raised eyebrows a generation earlier, this practice was becoming increasingly common
in the early 1970s. Many young couples considered this a relatively painless way to determine each other's compatibility before com-
mitting to marriage. However, the practice of sharing living quar-
ters also reflects to a considerable degree the more permissive
moral standards embraced by the "hippie" culture of the '60s.

Hillary and Bill also teamed up to campaign for Sen. George
McGovern, a Democrat who in 1972 was running for president
against Republican incumbent Richard Nixon. The pair flew to
Texas to put their energies and talents to work on behalf of the liberal senator, but his campaign turned out to be a losing proposition. Nixon, promising to bring a swift end to the Vietnam War,
won another four years in the White House by an overwhelming
margin. As it turned out, the war continued to drag on despite the
president's assurances to the contrary, and Nixon's reelection triumph ended up being one of the few highlights of his second term.

After the campaign, Hillary renewed her focus on children, particularly what she perceived as their appalling lack of legal rights in the United States. Working through Yale's Child Study Center, she researched children's rights in society and the court system. She would go on to write three articles in the next several years, published in the *Harvard Educational Review*, the *Yale Law Journal*, and an academic series called *Children's Rights: Contemporary Perspectives.*

Hillary felt government should refrain from interfering in family affairs unless failure to do so would put children at risk. She also suggested that children be allowed to make decisions earlier than the ages of 18 or 21, the ages at which minors are legally recognized in many states as capable of making decisions affecting their future. In one way or another, children would continue to be the focus of much of her work in the following years, even after she reached the White House.

Hillary stayed on an extra year at Yale and graduated in 1973 with Bill. They chose different career paths than most of their peers, who would end up earning large salaries at prosperous law firms. In Judith Warner's biography of Hillary, a classmate said, "Everyone was ambitious. But I see Bill and Hillary as driven by almost a religious purpose of some sort. They had the sort of late sixties' sense of 'we have to make the world better.' Not 'I have to make the world better,' but 'we,' all people, acting together."

As he had always planned, Clinton promptly returned to his home state and took a job teaching at the University of Arkansas Law School. Meanwhile, Hillary resumed working for the Children's Defense Fund in Cambridge, Massachusetts, which advocated and defended children's rights.

But six months later, Hillary Rodham was among a select group of young Yale law students (including Bill Clinton) invited to work for John Doar, the special counsel to the House Judiciary Committee. He wanted five law school graduates who weren't afraid of hard work, much of it behind the scenes, poring over stacks of documents. The congressional panel was conducting an inquiry and hearings to determine if there were grounds to remove President Nixon from office. He and members of his administration were under intense media and political scrutiny for their roles in a 1972 burglary of Democratic National Headquarters at the Watergate Apartments building in Washington. Throughout the inquiry, the president denied any knowledge of or personal involvement in the bungled attempt to steal campaign secrets from the Democrats.

Nonetheless, the Judiciary Committee was determined to discover if the president had indeed had a hand either in the affair or in attempts to cover it up afterwards. Hillary was one of 44 attorneys recruited to research whether Nixon's role justified impeachment (removal from office), and if so, how it would be conducted. Meanwhile, Bill Clinton had declined the invitation to work on the legal team.

Most of Hillary's work involved establishing the legal steps to follow during the inquiry and impeachment, labor that required ground-level attorneys like herself to spend as much as 20 hours a day studying legal precedents and the Constitution itself. She also was privileged to hear audio tapes of the president's intimate White House conversations; this was highly sensitive information. "I was kind of locked in this soundproof room with the big headphones on, listening to tapes," Hillary later told the *Arkansas Gazette*. "There was one we called the tape of tapes. It was Nixon taping himself listening to the tapes, making up his defenses to what he heard on the tapes. So you would hear Nixon talk and then you'd hear very faintly the sound of a taped prior conversation with Nixon, [his top aides Bob] Haldeman, and [John] Ehrlichman . . . And you'd hear him say, 'What I meant when I said that was . . .' I mean, it was surreal, unbelievable. At

*Hillary congratulates her husband, the newly elected Attorney General of Arkansas.*

one point he asked Manuel Sanchez [his valet], 'Don't you think I meant this when I said that?'"

The team's task was to draw up three articles of impeachment based on obstruction of justice, abuse of power, and contempt of Congress. Ultimately, Nixon saved himself and the country the embarrassment of impeachment proceedings by resigning on August 8, 1974. His vice president, Gerald Ford, assumed the helm of power but would lose a narrow reelection bid two years later to Jimmy Carter, a southern Democrat who was the governor of Georgia.

Hillary considered her experience on the legal panel "one of the greatest personal and professional opportunities I've ever had. . . . The staff that was put together was so professional, experienced. I was just a fresh, young law school graduate, and I got to work with these people, and it was such an historic experience." At this point in her life, she had proved she was as skilled a lawyer as she had been a student and could have had her pick of jobs in several major Washington law firms. However, Hillary now found herself agonizing over the direction to take next. If her logical, orderly mind told her to pursue an independent law career with the promise of a hefty salary and advancement, she must have ignored the message. Instead, she had a friend drive her to Fayetteville, Arkansas, where a pining Bill Clinton had invited her more than once.

Through a contact at the same University of Arkansas Law School where Bill was teaching, Hillary landed a job as associate professor of criminal law. She had already taken the bar exam—a test given by each state certifying a lawyer can practice law in that state.

Bill Clinton decided in August of 1974 to run for office, seeking to represent Arkansas's Third District in the U.S. House of Representatives. A supportive Hillary Rodham contributed $400 to the race. More important, she took on the role of unofficial campaign manager and promptly whipped the poorly organized effort into shape. Even her brothers and Hugh and Dorothy Rodham were recruited to pitch in.

Clinton displayed his considerable skills as well, one of which was soliciting money. He raised the then-remarkable amount of $50,000 to fill his campaign war chest. Even so, he lost the race, partly because he was up against a powerful Republican incumbent and partly because his draft record had become an issue.

Despite the loss, Hillary Rodham apparently felt content in Arkansas, which is remarkable in itself considering how different the state was from her suburban Chicago home. Someone once said Arkansas has two classes: the rich and the poor. Although blessed with beautiful scenery in some areas, the state routinely finished dead last nationwide in quality of education, and it had a legendary reputation for political corruption and catering to big-monied interests. In few other states were the spoils of the land and government divvied up among so few.

Hillary continued her quest for career opportunities, even stopping at a Marine recruiting post to inquire about signing on. Said a female recruiter: "You're too old, you can't see, and you're a woman. Maybe the dogs [U. S. Army] would take you."

Her uncustomary indecisiveness led Hillary to travel and visit friends in several major U.S. cities, where she hoped to find inspiration for her future. After several weeks, however, she returned to Fayetteville. Years later, she would confess to a writer: "Bill's desire to be in public life was much more specific than my desire to do good."

Unbeknownst to her, Bill bought a small house—his way of proposing to Hillary. "Well, I thought you liked it, so I bought it," he reportedly told her after picking her up at the airport. "So I guess we'll have to get married now." Which they did, on October 11, 1975, in their own cottage. Dorothy Rodham later told a magazine, "It was just a little, tiny house, only worth a handful of money. I think there were only two rooms." Nonetheless, she was touched by the couple's earnestness, she would also relate. "To see these two brilliant students loaded with diplomas, which could have brought them all the luxury and money in the world, there in Arkansas, in that modest house because they had dreams of realizing their ideals. It was so moving."

Hillary Rodham told friends she intended to keep her maiden name, something she had decided to do even as a young girl.

Meanwhile, the newlyweds had precious little time to celebrate their nuptials; soon afterward, both signed on to work on Jimmy Carter's 1976 bid for the presidency. Bill steered the campaign in Arkansas, while his

new wife became Carter's deputy director in nearby Indiana. This campaign turned out to be a winning Democratic effort, and in gratitude for Hillary's assistance the new president from Plains, Georgia, eventually appointed her to the national board of the Legal Services Corporation, a public organization that provided legal services to the needy. Serving on the board with her was Mickey Kantor, who 16 years later would guide Bill Clinton's first campaign for the presidency.

But in 1976, the man from Hope had his eye on the Arkansas attorney general's post, essentially the state's top legal prosecutor. And, as in his first race, Hillary was again at his side, organizing and advising while she juggled teaching legal classes and freelance legal work. Their fundraising and organizational teamwork paid off; Clinton won handily, garnering 60 percent of the votes in the May 1976 primary and running unopposed in the fall general election. He had not yet turned 30 years old.

*Hillary became one of the few female attorneys working for a major law firm in Arkansas when she joined the Rose Law Firm in 1977. This is the firm's headquarters in Little Rock.*

Early in 1977, Hillary and Bill left Fayetteville and moved to Little Rock to live in the state capital. Not content to simply be the wife of the attorney general, Hillary Rodham eagerly accepted a position with the Rose Law Firm, arguably the most influential legal practice in the state. It had been founded a century and a half earlier by U. M. Rose, who also was instrumental in starting the American Bar Association. During the firm's history, six Rose lawyers had left to serve as justices on the Arkansas Supreme Court. Hillary was one of only a few women in Arkansas working as a lawyer for a major firm.

In the next year, she helped start Arkansas Advocates for Children and Families, the state's first nonprofit organization advocating legal rights for children. The group targeted problems like teenage pregnancy, drug and alcohol abuse, and poverty. Hillary had never understood why children in America were afforded few legal rights, arguing on one occasion that the courts hadn't kept up with the times. "This attitude is especially prominent in regard to the labeling of certain behavior as delinquent," she wrote, referring to behavior like truancy, sexual promiscuity, and running away. Such an attitude "represents a confused mixture of social control and preventive care that has resulted in the confinement of thousands of children for the crime of having trouble growing up."

Most of all, Hillary Rodham wanted children to have many of the same rights granted adults, and she also fought to assure them good nutrition, a healthy home environment, and emotional well-being. Thanks to her efforts on children's behalf, and other trial work outside the Rose Law Firm, she developed a reputation as a compassionate, effective trial attorney.

Bill Clinton had spent barely 14 months in the attorney general's office when he trained his sights on another political position—governor of Arkansas. His 1978 campaign for governor was well organized, well

financed, and strategically run from locations all across the state. Clinton raised over half a million dollars for his campaign, three times more than any previous gubernatorial candidate had amassed. The effort paid off as Clinton won the spring primary against four lesser opponents by a 60 percent margin, a lead he would surpass by still more in the November election. He became Arkansas's second-youngest governor in January 1979 at age 32.

He took the oath of office with Hillary Rodham at his side holding the Bible. Reflecting the more unconventional nature of the new governor and first lady, guests were invited to wear "diamonds and denim" at the inaugural ball afterward. Inside a brooch worn by Hillary was a huge diamond that had been mined in Arkansas's Crater of Diamonds State Park. (Arkansas is the only state in the nation where diamonds have been discovered.) She also wore a gown created by a Little Rock

*Hillary Rodham helped organize a successful gubernatorial campaign for her husband in 1978, and at age 32, Bill Clinton was sworn in as Arkansas's governor with his proud wife by his side.*

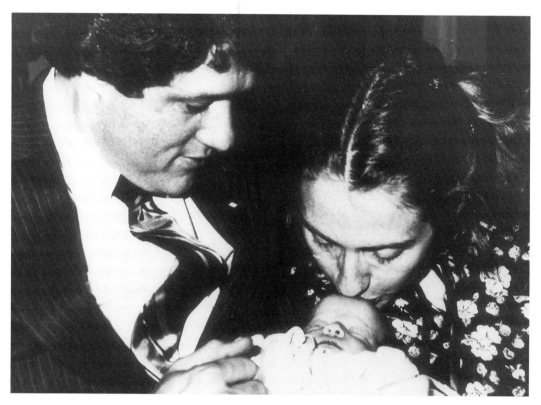

*One of the highlights of the Clintons' first term in office was the birth of their daughter, Chelsea, on February 27, 1980. Hillary maintained her legal career and assisted her husband's political career while taking care of their child.*

designer and embellished with trim and embroidery from dresses worn by Arkansas women a century earlier.

Although careful for appearances' sake to be every bit Arkansas's first lady, Hillary also made no pretense about retaining her own name—and separate career—telling the public, "We realized that being a governor's wife could be a full-time job. But I need to maintain my interests and my commitments. I need my own identity too."

Not surprisingly, however, many Arkansas voters were beginning to question their first lady's independent leanings. Soon after moving into the governor's mansion, she felt obliged to justify the name decision, telling the *Arkansas Democrat*: "I made speeches in the name of Hillary Rodham. I had taught law under that name. I was, after all, 28 when I married, and I was fairly well established."

So much so, in her husband's opinion, that he promptly named her to head the state's Rural Health Advisory Committee, a board charged with developing better health-care delivery to residents in outlying parts of Arkansas. Despite the increasing scrutiny of the first lady, the appointment failed to generate ripples, unlike a remarkably similar move years later in the White House. Still, from the very first, Hillary's plain-Jane appearance, including her headbands and horn-rimmed glasses, didn't endear her to the people of Arkansas, especially after she was spotted at a spirited college football game reading a book while her husband cheered enthusiastically for the Arkansas Razorbacks.

One development that did generate warm feelings toward Hillary and Bill was the announcement that their first child was on the way. The couple had been trying to have a baby for several years, and their dream was finally realized on February 27, 1980, when Chelsea Victoria Clinton was born three weeks prematurely. The Clintons reveled in the birth and set out to become model parents.

The governor took credit for settling on his daughter's name, Hillary would tell *Newsweek* magazine. "It was this glorious morning. We were going to brunch and we were walking through Chelsea [England]—you know, the flowerpots were out and everything. And Bill started singing, 'It's a Chelsea morning,' the Judy Collins song."

In *It Takes A Village*, Hillary wrote that she had read all the books on parenting she could get her hands on during her pregnancy, but "infants don't come with handy sets of instructions," she noted wryly. Hillary also reminisced that only a generation earlier, America's larger extended families had always helped new mothers make the delicate transition to parenthood. Today, there are plenty of books and devices, she observed, but few "people and programs to help fledgling parents."

And as the family's "designated worrier," she was

determined to protect and nurture Chelsea just as her own mother had when Hillary was growing up in Chicago. Hillary later admitted she didn't want to look back on her daughter's upbringing with regret for time lost. "As the saying goes, 'no one on his deathbed ever says he wishes he'd spent more time at the office,'" she wrote. "Many divorced men who form second families vow they won't neglect their children the second time around. But children from a first marriage aren't training wheels, and they don't get a second chance at childhood."

At the same time, Hillary juggled the demands of motherhood with a career—successfully so, it seems. The same year her daughter was born, she became a partner in the Rose Law Firm. Furthermore, Hillary convinced the firm to grant her a four-month maternity leave (unheard of at the time) even though she drew "a lot of blank stares" when she inquired about it. "[Most] new parents don't meet with anything like this kind of accommodation," she noted over a decade later.

Unfortunately, Bill Clinton's once promising career had fallen on hard times. He had accomplished little of what he had set out to do in his first term, including an early plan to dismiss incompetent teachers and require all new ones to pass a standard competency test before being certified. The same legislation also called for mandatory achievement tests for all students in three grades each year. After a firestorm of criticism, the governor withdrew the proposed bill. In addition, Governor Clinton had riled the electorate by raising driver's registration fees to pay for road repairs, a move that cost him considerable support. Moreover, people had grown weary of the governor's "long-haired" advisors and had never forgiven the first lady for keeping her maiden name even after having a baby. The final blow was President Jimmy Carter's decision to relocate some 19,000 Cuban boatlift refugees to a federal holding area at Fort Chaffee in northwest Arkansas. After being cooped up in the camp during one of the hottest sum-

*A pensive Bill Clinton and his wife watch as the votes are counted during the 1980 gubernatorial election. Clinton failed in his reelection bid and was devastated by the loss.*

mers in Arkansas's recent history, several hundred refugees broke out of the compound and briefly marched toward a nearby town.

The governor's Republican opponent, Frank White, took advantage of the misadventure, running television ads that all but said Bill Clinton had invited Cuba's criminals and outcasts to his home state by not refusing Carter's relocation order. Combined with a series of other embarrassing mistakes and the public's displeasure with Bill's tax increases and Hillary's feminism, the Clinton reelection effort continued to flounder. In the end, Bill lost his bid for a second gubernatorial term by over 30,000 votes. The loss devastated him for six months, friends said, and led to one of the most trying times in the young couple's marriage.

*Bill and Hillary Clinton share a tender moment during his 1992 presidential campaign.*

# 6

# THE ROAD TO
# THE WHITE HOUSE

Thanks in large part to Hillary, her husband's political career wasn't nipped in the bud. As he set out through the Arkansas countryside literally asking people on the street where he'd gone wrong, she took stock of the contempt many people in Arkansas held for her and came to a painful conclusion: something had to change. During a kickoff for Clinton's 1982 campaign to regain the governor's seat, the former first lady of Arkansas announced that she intended in public to refer to herself as Mrs. Bill Clinton, reserving her maiden name for work she might do for the Rose Law Firm, from which she had taken a leave of absence.

News of her announcement swept not just through Arkansas, but across the country, putting her in the uncomfortable position of having to defend her decision. She told one newspaper that her maiden name had interfered with people's perception of the kind of job her husband had done. "I did not want to have made a decision which would impact adversely on what he had chosen to be his life's work," she said. "After thinking about it a lot and seeking a lot of guidance, I became Hillary Rodham Clinton."

Although she publicly downplayed the importance of retaining her name as a badge of independence, many of her friends felt Hillary had made a major concession, albeit one she had little choice but to make. Remarkably, the same critics who had given her so much grief in Arkansas suddenly had a change of heart and began to embrace her softened image. The public actually began to like the new Mrs. Bill Clinton, who had also lightened and styled her hair, shed the headbands, and forsaken horn-rimmed glasses for contact lenses.

Her husband, in turn, trimmed his long hair and surrounded himself with older, more clean-cut campaign staffers than he had employed in the past. In addition, he kicked off his latest campaign with this apology: "If you'll give me a second chance to serve again, you'll have a governor who has learned from defeat that you can't lead without listening."

Through their combined efforts, the repackaged couple turned an uphill reelection bid into a sweeping victory, and they moved back into the Little Rock executive mansion resolving not to repeat past mistakes.

Not long after regaining the governorship, Bill Clinton turned to his wife to lead a new task force designed to improve Arkansas's woeful education system. The first lady's appointment raised few objections, and she launched the Arkansas Education Standards Committee with typical fervor by speaking at rallies across the state. At one in particular, she said, "We expect nothing but the best from our athletes: discipline, teamwork, standards. I wish we could translate the same expectations and standards we have for athletics into the classroom. I wish we could give teachers the same support and praise for teaching children to read and write as we do those who teach them to throw a ball through a hoop."

In an interview with the *Arkansas Democrat*, she took a stance remarkably similar to one her husband would embrace years later when pushing for education reform nationwide. "One of the principal problems we face in our state, and apparently in the country, is that we are not expecting enough of ourselves, our schools, or our students," said Hillary. "We have an obligation to challenge our students and to set high expectations for them. Rather than setting minimum standards, we should set expectations and urge schools and districts to aim to achieve those expectations and not to be satisfied with meeting some artificial minimum."

After nine months of grueling work, Hillary Rodham Clinton presented the committee's findings to the Arkansas legislature. With husband Bill looking on from the wings, she delivered the group's recommendations, which were to be funded with an increase in the state sales tax. The education reforms included competency exams for third-, sixth-, and eighth-graders and required teens to stay in school until age 17. Competency tests for teachers, which drew the wrath of Arkansas's public school teachers' union, were also part of the reform package. After hours of discussion, the legislators broke out into applause for her presentation, and state representative Lloyd George said, "I think we've elected the wrong Clinton."

Although the legislative changes the report initiated drew mixed reviews (10 percent of Arkansas teachers, a large number of them African American, failed the first competency test), Hillary won praise for her efforts, including an award from the Arkansas Press Association. In addition, she sparked the state to establish a Home Instruction Program for Preschool Youngsters, also known as HIPPY. Based on a program developed decades earlier in Israel, HIPPY encourages parents to take responsibility for their children's early education at home.

Hillary later told an author: "Half of all learning occurs by the time a person is five. There are instances, each of us knows, where people from very terrible situations rise above them and do well. But those are the exceptions, and most people who have the kind of impoverished, often neglectful backgrounds that we see

*Hillary accepted that her plain image was part of the reason for Bill Clinton's election defeat, so she decided to soften her look. She also announced that she would no longer go by her maiden name, but would take her husband's last name.*

so often among many of our children today just come into school with so many problems that it's very difficult to deal with. So a good preschool program, whether it's center-based or home-based, is one of the smartest improvements."

The accolades for her efforts continued to grow. In 1984, she received the Public Citizen of the Year award from the Arkansas chapter of the National Association of Social Workers, and she was selected Woman of the Year in a poll by *Arkansas Democrat* readers. Hillary's success also didn't hurt Bill's standing, and the couple made the *Esquire* magazine list of people called "the best of the new generation."

By 1986, Hillary had become one of the most admired women in Arkansas, and was on top professionally as well. As a partner in the Rose Law Firm, she was making $100,000 a year, while her husband pulled down a comparatively meager $35,000 as chief executive of the state. She had become the first trial lawyer in Arkansas to examine a witness via satellite during a trial, and she won acclaim for convincing a judge to award custody of children to the father in a bitter court case.

A former associate who had worked under her at the Rose Law Firm told biographer Judith Warner he had been thoroughly impressed with Hillary's legal skills during the case. "I can still picture her standing there with her palms down on the table, getting ready to deliver her closing argument," he said. "It had just gotten dark outside, there were more spectators than usual in the courtroom, and you could've heard a pin drop. She delivered a closing argument that lasted fifteen or twenty minutes that was really emotional and extremely articulate. She didn't have notes, as usual for Hillary, and she never missed a beat. The judge ruled from the bench and granted a change of custody."

Offers to join boards and foundations or run commissions also flowed in. Hillary was asked to sit on the board of directors of Arkansas-based yogurt franchisee

*Hillary and Bill worked together to turn an uphill reelection battle into a victory and a return to the Arkansas gubernatorial mansion in 1982.*

TCBY Enterprises Inc. and retail powerhouse Wal-Mart. Also in 1986, she joined the William T. Grant Foundation Commission on Work, Family, and Citizenship to compile a study on "Youth and America's Future."

As if things weren't going well enough, Bill Clinton ran for another term as governor that year and was once again reelected, this time to a four-year term. The victory was due in no small part to his wife's stature and accomplishments, contributions he noted during his victory celebration. "I'm proud that she made this walk

*During Bill Clinton's second term as governor, he asked Hillary to lead a task force charged with improving public education in Arkansas. Hillary spoke at rallies across the state, advocating higher standards for both teachers and students. "We expect nothing but the best from our athletes," she said at one rally. "I wish we could give teachers the same support and praise for teaching children to read and write as we do those who teach them to throw a ball through a hoop."*

with me tonight," he said. "I think when the history of our state is written . . . no one will prove to have done more to advance the cause of our children and the future of this state than she has."

The Clintons would win another four-year term as governor and first lady of Arkansas in 1990. But by then, after 10 years in the state's executive mansion, Governor Clinton had firmly set his political sights on the executive mansion in Washington, D.C. Clinton had considered running for the presidency in 1988, but decided to postpone his campaign until the 1992 race. He announced his candidacy on October 3, 1991, spurred on by Mario Cuomo's decision not to run. Until then, New York's charismatic governor had been the apparent Democratic front-runner.

However, Bill Clinton soon found himself facing the

withering public scrutiny modern American presidential candidates must endure when they aim for the highest office in the land. Rumors of his previous marital infidelities ran rampant. As if that weren't troublesome enough, 12-year-old Chelsea Clinton also was drawn, unwittingly, into the limelight. She was a typical teen: tall, gangly, and sporting a set of braces. Nonetheless, Hillary was reportedly livid over the jokes and attention focused on Chelsea's appearance.

Determined to shore up the shaky foundation of her husband's candidacy, Mrs. Bill Clinton joined advisors James Carville and George Stephanopoulos in the campaign war room, devising responses to opponents' assaults and even anticipating crises before they arose. For example, the Clintons went public about their past marital "difficulties" before a group of assembled Washington, D.C., reporters.

In an often-quoted remark, Bill said: "What you need to know about me is that we have been together for almost 20 years and have been married almost 16, and we are committed to our marriage and its obligations, to our child and to each other. We love each other very much. Like anybody that's been together 20 years, our relationship has not been perfect or free of difficulties.

"But," he continued, "we feel good about where we are . . . And we intend to be together 30 or 40 years from now regardless of whether I run for president or not. And I think that ought to be enough."

The preemptive strike worked; the national media pegged Bill Clinton as the most electable Democratic candidate. But it was Hillary's composure and her ability to connect with voters that struck observers on the campaign trail. Some asked why she wasn't the one running for president, or at least some other prominent White House post.

Every ounce of her steely nerve was required for a second brush with the infidelity issue after a supermarket tabloid ran a story alleging an Arkansas nightclub singer, Gennifer Flowers, had conducted a 12-year affair with Bill. Determined not to buckle under to the unfavorable publicity, the Clinton election team agreed to a nationally televised interview on an episode of *60 Minutes*. It was a risky proposition, seeking to defend the governor's reputation before millions of Americans. The show was scheduled for broadcast immediately following the Super Bowl.

However, thanks to Hillary's courtroom finesse and unswerving support, the emotionally charged interview was a success. In it, she repeatedly expanded on her husband's answers when she felt them incomplete, and just as expertly closed the door on topics she felt too private to be aired on network television. "There isn't a person watching this who would feel comfortable sitting on this couch detailing everything that ever went on in their life or their marriage," she told CBS interviewer Steven Kroft. "And I think it's real dangerous in this country if we don't have a zone of privacy for everybody."

Once again, she had managed to douse a brushfire before it engulfed the Clinton candidacy. Unlike the reactionary campaign of Senator Gary Hart, who was woefully unprepared for the media spotlight focused on his extramarital life in 1988, the Clintons' strategy to go on the offensive and never leave a sling of mud unchallenged was paying off. The campaign picked up steam after a second-place showing in the New Hampshire primary, followed by sweeping victories in crucial southern primaries as well as in the Midwest. Bill Clinton had become the front runner for the Democratic party's presidential nomination, and national polls showed that the young govenor was cutting into incumbent Republican president George Bush's popularity among voters.

Nonetheless, the GOP (a term for the Republican party, meaning "Grand Old Party") refused to go quietly into the night. In a concerted effort to cripple the

*Although Hillary's partner-
ship in the Rose Law Firm
and her work for education
reform were very time-consuming, Hillary always
made time for her daughter.
This 1987 photo was taken
at one of Chelsea's soccer
matches.*

sometimes-inconsistent Clinton campaign, Republicans suddenly set their sights on Hillary, who was coming on a bit too strong in some people's opinion. Former Republican president Richard Nixon observed,
"Hillary pounds on the piano so hard that Bill can't be
heard. You want a wife who's intelligent, but not too

intelligent."

Her writings in college were attacked by conservative critics as advocating government's intrusion into family matters and giving children the right to sue their parents over minor disputes, an unfair conclusion easily dismissed by a closer reading of the positions she had actually endorsed. In addition, conservatives accused Hillary of being a radical feminist who was neither religious nor cared much about traditional family values.

The now-famous Whitewater story broke as well, outlining the Clintons' involvement in a failed Arkansas real estate development with partner James B. McDougal, who also oversaw a savings and loan institution that had become insolvent. Hillary's role in the affair drew particular attention because as a Rose Law Firm partner, she had performed what she described as "minimal" work for McDougal's defunct thrift, Madison Guaranty. Feeling compelled to defend her role in Whitewater, she denied having done anything wrong, adding, "I suppose I could have stayed home and baked cookies and had teas. But what I decided to do was pursue my profession, which I entered before my husband was in public life."

However, this line offended housewives around the country. Stunned by the overwhelming criticism for her remark, Hillary later expressed surprise at the harsh response it generated, telling a reporter, "I don't know how to feel about [the remark] . . . I think I'll just have to be more careful in the way I express my feelings, so I don't inadvertently hurt anybody. I can understand why some people thought that I was criticizing women who made different choices from the ones I had—in fact, criticizing the choice that my mother and a lot of dear friends have made. Nothing could be further from what I believe."

And in her book *It Takes A Village*, written in 1996 with the benefit of even more reflection, she said, "I had understood the question to refer to the ceremoni-

*During the 1992 Presidential Campaign, Hillary was often the focus of attacks by her husband's Republican opponents. However, her poise and unwavering support of her husband helped Bill Clinton win the election over incumbent President George Bush and third-party candidate Ross Perot.*

al role of a public official's spouse, and I replied that I had chosen to pursue my law practice while my husband was governor rather than stay home as an official hostess, serving tea and cookies. Now I've baked cookies and served tea, but I never thought that my cookie-baking or tea-serving abilities made me a good, bad, or indifferent mother, or a good or bad person. So it never occurred to me that my comment would be taken as insulting mothers (I guess including my own!) who chose to stay home with their children full time."

Chastened by the incident, much as she had been

*Hillary watches proudly as her husband is sworn in as the 42nd president of the United States.*

over the flap about her maiden name years earlier in Arkansas, Hillary took a breather from the campaign trail. She reemerged several months later, this time once again projecting a gentler image, typically blending campaign speeches with appearances emphasizing her maternal side.

The latest softening of her image evoked little sympathy from Republican strategists, who used the stage of their own national convention in August 1992 to deliver the harshest attacks yet on the first lady of Arkansas. Speaker Patrick Buchanan, epitomizing the ultraconservative wing of the GOP, eagerly took on the persona of pit bull. "Hillary believes that 12-year-olds should have the right to sue their parents. And Hillary has compared marriage and the family as institutions to slavery and life on an Indian reservation," he told the assembly. "Well, speak for yourself, Hillary."

Marilyn Quayle, the wife of Vice President Dan Quayle, also took the opportunity behind the podium to criticize Bill Clinton's wife, saying, "Not everyone believes that the family was so oppressive that women could only thrive apart from it." President George Bush's wife, Barbara, on the other hand, stayed above the fray for the most part and was especially dismayed by Buchanan's biting remarks.

In the end, the Republican blitzkrieg that targeted Hillary misfired, leading her to later tell *Newsweek*: "People can overlook and ignore a whole lot of stuff that is thrown out into the atmosphere if they view it as irrelevant, tangential, or just downright stupid and nasty. If you don't have a view of the world that is bigger than yourself, if the only reason that you're doing something is to fulfill your own personal ambition, then you can't sustain a campaign against that kind of concerted attack."

Moreover, the GOP effort to portray her as some kind of feminist demon failed to convince the American public that Hillary was a career woman first and a wife and mother second. Speaking to a convention of business and professional women that summer, she said: "I am all of those things and I am more than the sum of the parts: I am me. I've refused as best as I can and will continue to refuse the kind of stereotyping that tries to strip from me or tries to strip from anyone your individual dignity and your identity, because what I want . . . is a community where we celebrate one another and where we recognize the complexity of who we are."

With Tennessee Senator Al Gore as his running mate, Bill Clinton ultimately did convince American voters to grant him his lifelong dream of occupying the White House. Their victory over George Bush and independent candidate Ross Perot, although garnering only 43 percent of the popular vote, brought an end to a 12-year Republican presidential reign. More important, however, the election gave Bill Clinton and

*Barbara Bush, wife of President George Bush, takes Hillary on a tour of what would become the Clinton's home for the next eight years—the White House.*

Hillary Rodham Clinton the opportunity to become the most powerful partners in the world.

Shortly after the Clintons moved into the White House in January 1993, biographer Judith Warner summed up the first lady and her seemingly unlimited potential:

Without a doubt, whatever she chooses to do will go down in history, because Hillary Clinton will radically change America's notion of what a first lady can accomplish. She is strong, independent, unapologetically assertive, an equal partner both privately and professionally in her marriage. She is the first woman to arrive at the White House with a background equal to her husband's, an independent career as developed as his, and professional experience in policy activism on a par with his advisers. She is the first to have her own professional power base in Washington; the first whose only real disqualification from being a Cabinet member is the fact of being the president's wife.

Indeed, Mrs. Clinton's resumé as first lady is filled with firsts: She was both the first Yale Law School graduate and the first attorney to become first lady. And by the time she and the president began a second four years in the White House, she had become the only first lady to lead a presidential commission, the first to speak in China, and the first to win a Grammy award.

*Hillary Rodham Clinton pages through the numerous forms that a pregnant woman would need to complete to receive medical assistance at a Minnesota clinic. Hillary was chosen by her husband to lead a committee that would design a plan providing medical coverage for all Americans while cutting red tape.*

# 7

# GREAT
# EXPECTATIONS

Although Hillary Rodham Clinton's visibility in the 1992 presidential campaign clearly diminished in the final months before the general election, few observers expected a woman possessing her assertiveness, ambition, and intellect to remain in the shadows indefinitely. They were right.

Even before the Clintons moved into the White House, the president-elect announced that Hillary would chair a task force charged with designing a national health-care plan that would feature medical coverage for everyone. To the people of Arkansas, the appointment was nothing new. But for the vast majority of Americans, the news was proof that the Clinton White House was indeed going to be a unique partnership. With a few notable exceptions, most first ladies had contented themselves with spearheading such benevolent projects as redecorating the White House (Jacqueline Kennedy), beautification (Ladybird Johnson), or drug awareness (Nancy Reagan). Clearly, Hillary and Bill Clinton had bigger plans.

The new president had seized on the health-care issue after Harris Wofford rode it to victory in his 1991 upset win over a heavily favored Republican candidate in the Pennsylvania senate race. And who could be a better point-person for Bill Clinton than Hillary, his most intimate and trusted advisor? She began meeting with Democratic friends—and likely Republican foes as well—on Capitol Hill to begin courting their support. The legislators were duly impressed, much as Arkansas legislators had been years earlier when she presented then-Governor Clinton's education reform package. "She walked in there and took command," Senator Bob Kerrey, who had run for the Democratic presidential nomination against her husband, told *Newsweek*.

The breadth of the first lady's influence became obvious in other ways as well. News accounts noted that she had more senior aides than the vice president. And it was through her insistence that a woman, Janet Reno, was ultimately named Attorney General (after two otherwise capable female candidates failed to make the cut due to criticism over their hiring of illegal immigrants as domestic help). She also urged the appointment of Donna Shalala, previously with the Children's Defense Fund, as Secretary of Health and Human Services.

The first lady's standing among the American people began to rise following her appointment to tackle health-care reform, and she actually surpassed her husband in popularity. In between moving into their new home and steering the task force through its infancy, she made concerted efforts to spend time with Chelsea by attending her soccer games, at the same time planning dinners for heads of state. By all appearances, Mrs. Clinton was everything an ideal '90s mother was expected to be.

Her job on health-care reform was gargantuan. In 1993, 37 million Americans had no health insurance and another 35 million had less than adequate coverage. Providing coverage to them, and simultaneously broadening other forms of care, was estimated to cost a minimum of $50 billion a year. At the same time, it was obvious that something had to be done about the spiraling costs of care, which at the time were estimated to be rising by $100 billion annually. Mrs. Clinton's job was to sell the reform package to a skeptical Congress and the American people.

The administration had imposed a 100-day deadline for a report to be prepared for Congress. The White House wanted to move quickly because administration officials feared anything less than a breakneck pace might allow natural opponents of health-care reform, such as the insurance and drug industries and the American Medical Association, to rally their forces and defeat any legislation. In the months that followed the inauguration, Mrs. Clinton crisscrossed the country attending meetings, gathering information, and lobbying for change in whatever form her task force might ultimately recommend.

In the early days of the health-care task force, polls showed reform had struck a chord with the American people, some of whom had seen insurance premiums escalate dramatically in recent years—or could not afford insurance coverage at all. And the public initially seemed to trust Mrs. Clinton more than they did her husband or anyone else who was lobbying for a minimum standard for universal health coverage.

On Capitol Hill, meanwhile, Democrats and Republicans alike jockeyed to appear in photo opportunities with her as she worked the corridors of power on behalf of health-care reform. "She reduces people to jelly," a White House aide told *Newsweek*, "because there's a contest to see who can suck up the most when she's in the room. It's just weird. I can't imagine it with any other public figure."

However, her task was increasingly complicated by the specter of current administration missteps and the ghosts of resurrected dealings in Arkansas. The tribulations ranged from the trivial—adverse publicity over Bill Clinton delaying air traffic at Los Angeles International

*Hillary's support helped Janet Reno become the first woman Attorney General.*

Airport while he received an expensive haircut from a trendy stylist on Air Force One—to the more controversial, starting with the abrupt firing of seven veteran employees in the White House travel office. The staffers attended to the comfort and feeding of the traveling White House press corps, scheduling flights and accommodations as well as providing technical assistance.

The seven were sacked, it turned out, after a close friend of the Clintons protested that a Little Rock, Arkansas, travel agency he partly owned was not allowed to bid on White House air charters. A subsequent government audit revealed several thousand dollars' worth of discrepancies in the travel office's finances, which was cited as the primary reason for the firings. White House insiders also suspected that the employees had leaked information to Republicans whose reign in the executive mansion had just ended.

But before the Little Rock travel agency, which had provided flights for the Clinton campaign team, could move into the office, the behind-the-scenes power struggle came to light and a national firm was instead put in charge. The Travelgate incident, as it came to be known, may have gone largely unnoticed in business-as-usual Arkansas; but in Washington, D.C., it gave a black eye to the new administration.

In September 1993, months after the health-care plan was to have been in Congress's lap, Hillary's task force finally presented its Health Security Act on Capitol Hill. Under it, poor people and those struggling to make ends meet would receive government-subsidized coverage, while business and industry would offer coverage for all employees. A central theme to the plan, which President Clinton had vowed from the start he would not surrender, was universal coverage. The task force's presentation to Congress was nationally televised, and although the Health Security Act drew mixed reviews, Mrs. Clinton was praised for her role in developing the legislation. Afterward, the White House

*First Lady Hillary Rodham Clinton speaks with Sen. Carol Mosley Braun, who in 1993 became the first black woman elected to the U.S. Senate.*

settled into the long and arduous task of trying to shepherd the bill through Congress.

The ambitious Health Security Act would have radically changed medical care in the United States. The bill's supporters praised the task force's attempt to slow the rapidly rising cost of health care and its promise of medical coverage for everyone. Critics of the Health Security Act complained that the 1,342-page bill was too confusing, that it would create a massive new government bureaucracy devoted solely to overseeing health care, and that millions of dollars of new taxes would have to be levied to pay the cost of universal health care. Another knock against the bill

*Hillary takes part in a meeting on health-care reform. Her committee's task was huge—providing medical coverage to the approximately 70 million people without it was estimated to cost more than $50 billion a year.*

was that health care would be "rationed," meaning people needing special medical treatment might have to wait for a doctor to become available under the national health plan, even if the treatment was necessary to save their lives.

In addition, some conservative Republicans were upset at the "secret" way in which the health-care reform bill was drafted because Hillary and her task force had held closed meetings while developing the legislation. Some analysts also felt the task force did not include members with essential medical, technical, financial, and legal skills to develop and implement such a massive program.

Health-care reform was an issue central to Bill Clinton's election campaign, and the Clinton administration continued to push for universal medical care. However, a scandal resurfaced that would move the public's focus away from health care reform—Whitewater.

In 1978, the Clintons had become partners with Jim

and Susan McDougal to develop land near the White River in Arkansas. Bill Clinton was governor of Arkansas at the time, and Hillary was working at the Rose Law Firm. The Clintons had maintained for years that they had lost money in the deal, nearly $70,000 by their reckoning. Muddying the affair was the fact that McDougal had dealings with Whitewater Development Corporation through his savings and loan, Madison Guaranty. Madison failed in 1989; this cost taxpayers $60 million and led to criminal charges against McDougal, of which he was acquitted. As it happened, Hillary Rodham Clinton had also represented McDougal's savings and loan on occasion, at one point intervening with a Clinton-appointed regulator on a questionable stock scheme that McDougal had proposed.

Further complicating the matter was a missing file detailing the Clintons' involvement in Whitewater that had been kept by White House deputy counsel Vincent Foster, a former partner in the Rose Law Firm along with Hillary and an intimate friend of the couple. Six months after the Clintons and Foster moved into the White House, Foster committed suicide in a Virginia park. The Whitewater file was taken from his office shortly after his death—inadvertently, claimed White House officials—but was ultimately turned over to investigators in the Justice Department. In addition, some later reports indicated the Rose Law Firm may have shredded documents from its own files that had been maintained by Foster.

Many Washington observers felt the president and first lady only compounded suspicions of their involvement in Whitewater, the Foster suicide, and other questionable affairs by giving varying accounts of events, stonewalling investigations, and all the while maintaining that their privacy was being invaded by a sensationalizing media.

Whitewater had indeed captivated the media's attention, causing it to raise questions such as: Did Bill Clin-

*Vincent Foster, a White House lawyer and close friend of the Clintons from Arkansas, was found dead in a Virginia park, an apparent suicide. His death was linked by some observers to the Whitewater scandal that involved the Clinton administration.*

ton and his wife commit any crimes in their Whitewater dealings, or were they simply poor overseers of an investment that went awry? Was Vincent Foster's suicide somehow connected with initial probes into Whitewater, and if so, how? By the spring of 1994, the quagmire resulting from this failed real estate deal threatened to immobilize the Clinton White House.

Mrs. Clinton found herself unwittingly preoccupied with Whitewater fallout, which took valuable time from her health-care reform mission. Each day, it seemed, brought new revelations and allegations. In addition, Associate Attorney General Webster Hubbell, one of the president's closest friends and a former managing partner of Rose, was accused by his old law firm of having overbilled clients. Moreover, congressional hearings into the matter, sought by Republicans gleeful over the White House misfortunes, had become all but a certainty. Half a dozen administration aides were subpoenaed to appear in federal court, including top presidential advisers such as deputy chief of staff Harold Ickes and Deputy Secretary of the Treasury Roger Altman. Presidential counsel Bernard Nussbaum, who had worked with Hillary on the Nixon impeachment years earlier, became the first casualty of Whitewater. Nussbaum had removed the Whitewater files from Foster's office after his death and was asked by the administration to step down.

The entire Whitewater ordeal was snowballing, threatening to sink the President's most ambitious initiatives as well as Hillary's stature with the American public. In the spring of 1994, *Newsweek* observed:

> Even some of her admirers in Washington are searching for deeper causes for her secrecy. Hillary was exceedingly ambitious for herself and her husband, and was the main family breadwinner for years. Reared in a thrifty home, married to a spouse with a casual attitude about money, she developed a perhaps excessive concern for her family's finances.

In the '80s, during the shakiest times in their marriage, her concern for financial security may have been even more urgent. The question now is whether any of those pressures led her to cross ethical lines in various legal and business deals—and whether she used her husband's role as governor of Arkansas to help her do so.

President Clinton rallied to his wife's defense, saying at a press conference, "I have never known a person with a stronger sense of right and wrong." At the same time, Mrs. Clinton went on the counterattack herself, attributing the brouhaha to an overzealous press, partisan attacks instigated by the Republican party, and the notoriously bloodthirsty climate in Washington. Foster's own shredded suicide note amounted to an indictment of the capital city, "where ruining people is considered sport."

Even so, the first lady admitted she "made some mistakes," including investing in Whitewater in the first place and keeping a veil of secrecy on information related to the Foster suicide and other internal traumas. Indeed, the perennial White House insistence on absolute privacy had time and again aroused public suspicion when full disclosure might have been the best course. "[A]s long as [the administration] hunkers down behind its stone wall," noted a March 1994 *Newsweek* article, "the rumor-mongers are free to exercise and exploit their lurid imaginations."

In that same issue, Mrs. Clinton granted an interview in which she responded to journalist Eleanor Clift's pointed questions about the first family's woes. She admitted being sad about the allegations she and her husband might have done something corrupt in their Whitewater dealings, but she felt comparisons to Watergate (the Nixon-era scandal) were "way overblown."

Mrs. Clinton also admitted that privacy was important to her. "[I have] been pulled kicking and screaming to the conclusion that if you choose to run for public office you give up any zone of privacy at all," Hillary

*Hillary Clinton testifies on her task force's health-care reform plan before a congressional committee. After public opinion turned against the original health plan, President Clinton decided to quit the fight rather than pass a scaled-down health-reform bill.*

said. "I get my back up every so often about even having to answer questions that I don't think are in any way connected with the fact that my husband is in public life. That's what's going to be concluded about all this—people are going to spend millions and millions of dollars and they're going to conclude we made a bad land investment."

Just when it looked like things couldn't get worse for the Clintons, the horizon darkened even more. The president's old friend Webster Hubbell resigned from the number-three post in the Justice Department over allegations that he overbilled clients while at the Rose Law Firm. Nine months later, he pleaded guilty to mail fraud and tax evasion for overcharging clients such as the Federal Deposit Insurance Corporation and the Resolution Trust Corporation.

Meanwhile, on a different front, it appeared the battle to enact sweeping health-care reform had been lost. By early fall of 1994, a full year after the president's blueprint for universal health insurance was unveiled before Congress, both houses had recessed without approving the kind of all-encompassing legislation on which Bill Clinton had mortgaged his presidency. Faced with the dismal prospect of accepting a slimmer version of health-care reform down the road, the president opted simply to walk away from the battlefield.

Finger-pointing was the order of the day for what was described as a blown opportunity of historic proportions. Some blamed the president, who had done nothing to improve his reputation as a mediocre policymaker. Others lumped a sizeable portion of the blame on Mrs. Clinton, whom several observers inside and beyond the White House criticized for adopting a "take-no-prisoners" strategy from day one, when a more moderate approach may have appeased special interests and still served the public good. Conservative Republican opponents, like media commentator Rush Limbaugh, also helped defeat the legislation with their exaggerated reports about its potential impact on middle-class Americans, and special interest groups spent millions on advertisements and campaigns opposing the Health Security Act.

In any event, the struggle had obviously taken its toll on the first lady. Halfway through the administration's term, instead of keeping her fingers on the pulse of White House appointments and policies, she withdrew to recuperate and ponder her future. According to close associates, she was exhausted by the health-care reform battle and embittered at the lost opportunity. Some observers predicted she would content herself with the more traditional duties of the first lady during the remainder of the president's term, such as entertaining heads of state. Others felt she might eventually devote herself to tried-and-true themes, such as promoting the health and welfare of children.

*Hillary Rodham Clinton proudly displays the Grammy Award she won for the audiotape of her book,* It Takes A Village, *in February 1997. "I didn't even know that Grammys were given to tone-deaf people," she joked after learning she had won the award.*

# 8

# IT TAKES
# A VILLAGE

In early 1995, Americans got a glimpse of a new Hillary Rodham Clinton when she returned to her alma mater, Maine South High School in Park Ridge. With no obvious agenda such as health-care reform to promote, the first lady merely addressed students and shared dessert with them at a nearby restaurant. And, perhaps with an eye toward the next presidential election, she revealed in an interview with *U.S. News & World Report* that her main goal now was to help her husband in any way possible, including playing a card game or simply being a sympathetic listener.

Despite the bitter defeat on health-care reform, she expressed interest in continuing the fight for better care for women, children, and families. The first lady also denounced what she saw as "a continuing erosion in the trust placed in our public leaders, often on matters that have nothing to do with public issues or the public good." She added, "Unless we all figure out how we're going to sustain a democracy in the information-overload age, I'm concerned about who will enter public life, who will stay in public life, [and] the quality of decisions that are made."

While such statements by Mrs. Clinton implied she intended to stand by her man and still remain involved in issues dear to her, they led some of her staunchest fans to question whether she had, in fact, quietly assumed a back seat in the Clinton presidency. In a 1995 *Ladies Home Journal* article, columnist Barbara Reynolds of *USA Today* wondered if the first lady was being punished for being a strong woman. Reynolds seemed to think so, noting that men who fail to deliver on large tasks such as overhauling health care are simply shifted to new assignments, whereas Mrs. Clinton appeared to have been put out to pasture.

Reynolds urged the first lady to resist her more subdued status and instead direct her considerable energy, power, and natural tendency toward advocacy on another front: improving the lot of neglected children in America. "With the same vigor she used on health-care reform, she should put together a comprehensive plan to save our country's children and use her influence to make it happen," said Reynolds. "In helping to free our children from life-draining circumstances, she will also free herself from forced irrelevancy, and give fresh strength to the women who see her as a figure of hope."

As a prominent figure, Hillary Rodham Clinton was continually the target of unsolicited advice—and endless comparisons to other first ladies. Early in 1995 in the *New Yorker*, Doris Kearns Goodwin, author of *No Ordinary Time: Franklin and Eleanor Roosevelt: The Home Front in World War II*, wrote an eerily insightful commentary on "Hillary's dilemma:"

> Eleanor Roosevelt broke one precedent after another. She was the first First Lady to hold press conferences, to testify before committees, to write a daily column, to fly a plane. And there was a backlash. But she was consistent: she didn't take an inside policymaker role. She traveled the country and was a voice for people who didn't have access to Washington. And after a while people respected her greatly.
>
> Eleanor's experience suggests that it's better for the

First Lady to play other roles than insider. That way, you build a constituency. From the moment Hillary took a policy role, I was anxious for her. There's always a shorthand image for public figures: L.B.J. showing his scar, Ford's clumsiness. For Mrs. Clinton, it's telling Congress what to do. It's hard to transform shorthand. But it can be done. What's still possible for her is to go around the country and listen. She might organize the trip around children's issues—that is her strength. But if she tries merely to shift her image and be a traditional First Lady, she'll lose all the people who supported her precisely because she is a modern woman. It's not about becoming Barbara Bush.

Goodwin and other well-wishers needn't have worried. A year later, Hillary Rodham Clinton's familiar role as advocate again emerged. This time, however, the banner she bore wasn't health-care reform, but motherhood, childrearing, and revitalization of the American family. The first lady wrote a book, *It Takes A Village: And Other Lessons Children Teach Us*, and promoted it nationally on an 11-city tour. The title was derived from an African proverb: "Each of us plays a part in every child's life: it takes a village to raise a child."

To Mrs. Clinton, this saying means that children will thrive "only if their families thrive and if the whole of society cares enough to provide for them." Although she admits today's extended family is widely dispersed and more likely to stay in touch by telephone, computer, and fax machine rather than live in the same house or town, the goal remains the same: maintaining a support network of family, friends, teachers, and clergy.

In the book, the first lady revealed a warm, maternal side of her personality. In one telling example, Hillary had wanted to have a child so badly that, after years of trying unsuccessfully to have a baby, she had scheduled an appointment with a fertility clinic only to become pregnant before her appointment. Following Chelsea's birth, she said she had a newfound appreciation for the words of writer Elizabeth Stone: "Making the decision to have a child—it's wondrous. It is to decide forever to have your heart go walking around outside your body."

Hillary added, "Parenthood has the power to redefine every aspect of life—marriage, work, relationships with family and friends. Those helpless bundles of power and promise that come into our world show us our true selves—who we are, who we are not, who we wish we could be."

Occasionally, "who we are" tended to be overprotective, Hillary freely admitted. After she felt a chill one day and told Chelsea to wear a sweater, her young daughter responded, "I don't feel cold, Mommy. Maybe you do, but I have a different thermometer."

Nonetheless, she and the President, despite their time-consuming careers, must have done a great deal right as parents. By most measures, Chelsea, who has chosen to attend Stanford University in California, has matured into a surprisingly poised, well-adjusted young lady. At her parents' insistence, she has been all but invisible since the Clintons first entered the White House in 1993. Considering how much negative media attention the first family has endured since then, the decision seems justified.

Still, the media has agreed to keep its distance from the first teen for the most part. Except for a few early snide remarks about Chelsea on television, she has been allowed to lead as normal a life as the daughter of the most powerful parents in the country can. Granted, she had unlimited access to the White House bowling alley and movie theater. Most of the time, however, she chose to attend the local movie house with friends, some of whom invited her for sleepovers and also spent the night at 1600 Pennsylvania Avenue. And according to *Time*, a group of Chelsea's friends were invited to celebrate her 16th birthday at Camp David by donning camouflage and playing paintball.

Unlike some other children who have grown up in

*Hillary and Chelsea Clinton during a visit to India. In addition to taking care of her own daughter, Hillary has always been concerned with the welfare of children and the family in the United States and around the world.*

the White House, Chelsea is neither afraid of her own shadow or a spoiled brat, say observers. Instead, she's been described as relaxed, friendly, and "informed without being a smarty-pants." Even the most vocal presidential critics "concede the Clintons have raised an exceptional child," noted *Time*.

Despite how well Chelsea has turned out, Mrs. Clin-

*In 1995, Hillary was one of five women named Mother of the Year by the National Mother's Day Committee.*

ton maintains that the demands on working parents in the '90s have reduced the time devoted to children to a bare minimum, a trend she feels must be reversed. "Work spills over into time that used to be reserved for family, leisure, and other pursuits. This is partly because businesses downsizing and other economic stresses have 'upsized' workloads, increased commutes and overtime, and wreaked havoc with our daily routines," she wrote in her book. "These changes take an emotional toll, too. The growing sense that little is stable or permanent in our lives—families, neighborhoods, jobs, or values—clouds our priorities. So many of us have become part of what Secretary of Labor

Robert Reich has called 'the anxious class,' for whom worrying is a way of life.

"American mothers, both those who stay at home and those who work outside it, spend less than half an hour a day, on average, talking with or reading to their children, and fathers spend less than 15 minutes . . . If we only stopped to listen to them for a few minutes, kids could tell us that we move too fast, for their good and ours."

One of Mrs. Clinton's favorite lines came from a predecessor, Jacqueline Kennedy Onassis, who said, "If you bungle raising your children, I don't think whatever else you do matters very much."

In the face of what she perceived as skyrocketing threats to children—alcohol, tobacco, sex, drugs, divorce, and neglect—Mrs. Clinton argued that America as a government and society wasn't doing "enough of what works." Her proof? One in five children lives in poverty, 10 million children don't have health care coverage, 7,000 youngsters die by homicide or suicide each year, and 25 percent of all children are born to unwed mothers. In addition, she noted that children living with only one parent or in stepfamilies are "two to three times as likely to have emotional and behavioral problems as children living in two-parent families."

To counter these threats to the American family, Mrs. Clinton advised single parents to maintain their children's routines—meals, school, play, and bedtime—at all costs. She also advocated, over a five-year period, removing 100,000 children from foster care families and adoption rolls by putting them back with their families or into adoptive families.

And as for children themselves, the first lady suggested higher standards, especially regarding discipline and academic performance, because the biggest hindrances to learning are low expectations of students and schools. "We owe it to [our children] to do what we can to better their lives every day—as parents and

*The first lady addresses those in attendance at the Fourth World Conference on Women in Beijing, China. Hillary led the U.S. delegation to the conference, which was sponsored by the United Nations.*

through the myriad choices we make as employers, workers, consumers, volunteers, and citizens. We owe it to them to set higher expectations for ourselves," she says. "We must stop making excuses for why we can't give our children what they need at home and beyond to become healthy, well-educated, empathetic, and productive adults."

*It Takes A Village* not only was a hit with readers, but also received critical acclaim, with the recorded version winning the first lady a spoken-word Grammy award. After learning of the recognition, a delighted Mrs. Clinton cracked, "I didn't even know that Grammys were given to tone-deaf people."

The first lady's importance as a role model for women was strengthened when she was selected as honorary chairperson of the U.S. delegation to the Fourth World Conference on Women, held in China in the summer of 1996. The United Nations conference, which had been controversial from the start because of China's atrocious record on human rights, appeared to be barely tolerated by the Chinese government in Beijing, and it had all the makings of a public relations disaster for the White House. However, Mrs. Clinton turned out to be an appropriate choice to head the U.S. delegation because the agenda issues of young girls' rights and women in poverty were familiar themes for her. Over 25,000 delegates attended the event and heard Hillary deliver a powerful speech condemning human-rights abuses.

"Women of the world want to get a look at her," Joan Dunlop of the International Women's Health Coalition told *Newsweek* before the conference. "She has almost perfect pitch on these issues. Women genuinely admire her."

*William Rehnquist, Chief Justice of the Supreme Court, administers the presidential oath to William J. Clinton after his 1996 reelection triumph, as Hillary and Chelsea watch.*

# 9

# WHAT THE FUTURE HOLDS

Hillary Rodham Clinton's popularity with the American people as a role model was on the rise at the right time—just as her husband's presidential reelection campaign began in earnest.

Oddly enough, Mrs. Clinton would share the spotlight during the 1996 presidential campaign with another admired woman who was one of perhaps a handful of American women with a résumé as impressive as hers. That person was Elizabeth Dole, a former cabinet secretary to two presidents, the president of the American Red Cross, a Harvard-educated lawyer, and the wife of Senate Majority Leader Robert Dole, whom the Republicans hoped could unseat Bill Clinton.

The press naturally drew comparisons between Mrs. Clinton and Mrs. Dole because both were raised as staunch Methodists and came from well-to-do families but married men from modest beginnings. But for all they had in common on paper, the two were actually very different. For starters, Republican Elizabeth Dole had formerly been a Democrat, just the opposite of Hillary's transition. Moreover, Mrs. Dole had used her Harvard law degree to develop a lucrative career, just as Hillary could have done with her Yale degree had she not hitched her star to Bill Clinton. Therefore, Mrs. Dole had made her professional mark long before she fell in love with and married her husband. She also had never had a child, nor, short of her Red Cross work, been identified with Mrs. Clinton's more liberal advocacy. Her constituency in nearly three decades of government service had primarily been consumers.

Distinguishing the two women further was that the somewhat older Mrs. Dole was a product of her genteel Southern upbringing. This does not mean she wasn't ambitious or focused; she just had a more gracious way of getting what she wanted. Mrs. Clinton, thought to be the more impulsive of the two powerful women, has occasionally grated on the public nerve for appearing at times to rule the roost, even if only behind closed doors in the White House.

On the other hand, were it not for Hillary Rodham Clinton's involvement in every facet of her husband's political life, he may not ever have won a second gubernatorial race in Arkansas, overcome the infidelity hurdle and other attacks on his character, or been elected president. Without such a caring, protective partner as Hillary by his side, one can only speculate how his career might have evolved in the relative obscurity of Arkansas politics.

Despite Republican attacks on the Clinton administration because of its many scandals, the public apparently was happy with the direction the nation was headed. In November 1996, Bill Clinton won 49 percent of the vote to 41 percent for Bob Dole. The race was never really close. Third-party candidate Ross Perot received the other eight percent of the vote.

While Mrs. Clinton's book, subsequent honors like the Grammy, and her prominent role on the world stage provided a welcome respite from inquiries into the scandal of the moment, the good times were usually soon overshadowed by some new twist or revelation

*Bill and Hillary Clinton—
the most powerful partners
in the world.*

that raised further suspicions about the administration.

There was, for instance, the remarkable discovery early into the second Clinton term of the first lady's Whitewater billing records. They had been sought by investigators for two years, and were only now noticed by a long-time aide in an old box of papers in an East Wing office. How they got there no one could quite say. But investigators pored over them because the documents contained numerous handwritten notes by the late Vincent Foster. More important, they seemed to indicate the first lady had understated her involvement to federal regulators concerning just how much work she had done for James McDougal, Madison Guaranty's owner and the Clintons' former Whitewater partner.

In the same week in 1996, the White House released details of a telling memo penned by former White House administrative chief David Watkins. It pointed an accusing finger directly at the first lady, suggesting Mrs. Clinton had masterminded the travel office firings after all. Congressional committees investigating the affair planned to question additional witnesses, as well as recall earlier ones who may not have been entirely forthcoming. Still, no charges were levied against the Clintons accusing them personally of wrongdoing.

Shortly before Christmas 1996, the First Lady, apparently weary of attacks on her behavior in office during the victorious yet bruising presidential campaign, revealed just how difficult life can be as a '90s woman in a job perhaps more suited to a 19th-century lady. "This position is such an odd one," Mrs. Clinton said to a crowd of prominent Australian women listening to her speak on a state visit. "In our country we expect so much from the woman who is married to the president—but we don't really know what it is we expect.

"There is something about the position itself which raises in Americans' minds concerns about hidden power, about influence behind the scenes, about unaccountability," added the first lady. "Yet if you try to be public about your concerns and your interests, then that is equally criticized. I think the answer is to just be who you are and do what you can do and get through it—and wait for a First Man to hold the position."

A *Time* article in which her remarks appeared summed up Mrs. Clinton's dilemma better than most: ". . . in truth, this First Lady is still trying to figure out who she can be and what she can do. She does not want to repeat the mistakes she made during her husband's first two years in office, when she alienated many Americans not because she was a powerful woman but because she seemed not to realize that the citizenry expects its powerful leaders, male and female, to show the humility befitting those whose authority is merely on loan from the people."

In a pensive interview with Mrs. Clinton on the Australian visit, *Time* wondered what the first lady had learned in her last four difficult years. "I'm sure there are lots and lots of lessons, things we did that could have been done better," Mrs. Clinton said without acknowledging any in particular. "It's hard to look back, because I know so much more now than I did on Jan. 20, 1993 . . . There is nothing to prepare you for walking into the White House. I've learned so much I can't even begin to digest it all."

Although few modern presidential administrations have escaped scandal—Watergate, Richard Nixon's Achilles heel; Iran-Contra, Ronald Reagan's botched arms-for-hostages scheme—the Clinton White House finds itself subject to an unprecedented number of ethical and criminal inquiries. The Whitewater investigation continues to broaden in scope, with an independent counsel, Kenneth W. Starr, charged with uncovering what, if any, illegal activity had taken place, and who was responsible.

In April 1997, the *Los Angeles Times* reported that Starr had found "extensive evidence" of a possible cover-up in the probe involving the president and first lady. He sought and was granted an extension of the Whitewater grand jury investigation. Specifically, the grand jury was probing the validity of accusations that the President had lied about his activities in the Whitewater case, that administration officials may have arranged "hush money" for former Associate Attorney General Webster L. Hubbell, and "that someone close to the president concealed records of the legal work that First Lady Hillary Rodham Clinton did for Whitewater conspirator James B. McDougal's savings and loan," said the newspaper.

McDougal had previously defended the first couple's involvement in his ventures. But in exchange for cooperating with Starr's investigation, his sentence on con-

*During the second term of the Clinton administration, Hillary Rodham Clinton and her husband remained beset by scandals, most notably the investigation into Whitewater.*

spiracy and fraud charges had been reduced. McDougal, who had earned a reputation for being erratic at times, now told the *Times* he "got sick and tired of lying" for Clinton.

Another controversy erupted on the Whitewater front: the Associated Press reported in May 1997 that the White House and Whitewater investigators had been secretly battling over access to notes of conversations between the First Lady and White House attorneys. A federal appeals court had ordered the White House to turn over two sets of notes to Starr's team of investigators. But citing claims of executive privilege, President Clinton authorized an appeal to the U.S. Supreme Court.

The subpoenaed notes in question concern Mrs. Clinton's discussions with White House lawyers about her role in events following Vincent Foster's death and the misplaced, then rediscovered, Whitewater billing records. The White House claimed the first lady's conversations were protected by the same confidences afforded clients with their private attorneys. But the federal panel of judges saw differently, noting in their ruling, "An official who fears he or she may have violated the criminal law and wishes to speak with an attorney in confidence should speak with a private attorney, not a government attorney."

A White House lawyer said the administration's refusal to turn over the notes was not based on hiding information, but preserving "this president's and future presidents' ability to seek candid and confidential legal advice," the Associated Press reported.

Less than two weeks later, the Whitewater prosecutors and White House lawyers argued the merits of their case before the Supreme Court. Starr's team maintained the First Lady had changed her testimony from that given before a federal grand jury investigating Whitewater. White House lawyers insisted the lower federal appeals court had wrongly concluded that the subpoenaed notes were not protected by attorney-client privilege.

Mrs. Clinton herself filed a brief with the high court, arguing the appeals court ruling "disregards the compelling need for personal and governmental lawyers to consult." She described her plight "as a situation where a person with official responsibilities is under partisan attack and faces investigation by Congress, administrative agencies and one or more independent counsels."

According to recently released court papers, Starr considered the first lady "a central figure" in his probe, and alluded to extensive evidence of possible obstruction of his investigation, said the news story. Starr said the claims of privilege by the White House "had impeded his investigation for months."

In July 1997, the Supreme Court basically granted Starr access to the White House notes by declining to review the lower-court ruling. However, there are growing doubts the first lady will ever be publicly accused of any criminal wrongdoing in Whitewater, the travel office firings, the Foster suicide, or any other scandals involving the administration. And despite all the adverse publicity, Hillary Rodham Clinton continues to be viewed favorably by the American public.

During her career, Hillary Rodham Clinton has held many positions: advocate, policymaker, supportive wife, and mother. She has always played an important role as a political partner to Bill Clinton and will likely do so for the remainder of his presidency. After her husband leaves office, what will be the next challenge for this ambitious, modern woman? Hillary could continue her advocacy for children's rights and family values and remain a role model for women. She could return to her legal career, be appointed a judge, or even decide to run for public office herself. One thing is certain: Hillary Rodham Clinton has redefined the role of America's first lady, and in so doing has broadened the opportunities for women everywhere.

*Hillary Rodham Clinton ponders her future while strolling on the beach in North Carolina. Hillary, like no previous first lady, has redefined the position and become a role model for women everywhere.*

# FURTHER READING

Brock, David. *The Seduction of Hillary Rodham*. New York: The Free Press, 1996.

Clinton, Hillary. *It Takes A Village: And Other Lessons Children Teach Us*. New York: Simon & Schuster, 1996.

King, Norman. *Hillary: Her True Story*. Secaucus: Birch Lane Press, 1993.

Morris, Roger. *Partners in Power, The Clintons and Their America*. New York: Henry Holt & Co., 1996.

Renshon, Stanley A. *High Hopes: The Clinton Presidency and the Politics of Ambition*. New York: New York University Press, 1996.

Warner, Judith. *Hillary Clinton, The Inside Story*. New York: Penguin Books, 1993.

Woodward, Bob. *The Agenda: Inside the Clinton White House*. New York: Simon & Schuster, 1994.

1947    Born Hillary Diane Rodham on Oct. 26, in Chicago, Illinois.

1960    Began her first job, at age 13, supervising children in a summer park program.

1962    Met Martin Luther King Jr. at Chicago's Orchestra Hall while with her Methodist Church Youth Group led by Rev. Donald Jones.

1965    Graduated from Maine South High School 15th in her class of 1,000, a National Merit Scholarship Finalist, student council leader, and member of National Honor Society. Voted girl "Most Likely to Succeed."

1969    Was first student ever chosen to deliver commencement speech at Wellesley College in Boston, where she majored in political science. Was accepted at Yale Law School.

1970    Began working for Marian Wright Edelman, founder of the Washington Research Project, and met future husband William Jefferson Clinton.

1973    Graduated from Yale Law School with Bill Clinton.

1974    Began working with House Judiciary Committee's counsel to draw up articles of impeachment against President Richard M. Nixon.

1975    Married Bill Clinton Oct. 11 in Fayetteville, Arkansas.

1977    Moved to Little Rock, Arkansas, after Bill was elected state Attorney General, and went to work for the Rose Law Firm.

1978    Became first lady of Arkansas when Bill was elected governor, and was appointed to head Rural Health Advisory Commission.

1980    Gave birth to daughter Chelsea Victoria Clinton on Feb. 27, and became a partner in Rose Law Firm.

1982    Announced she'll go by Mrs. Bill Clinton or Hillary Rodham Clinton as Bill kicks off third race for governor.

1984    Won Public Citizen of the Year Award from Arkansas chapter of National Association of Social Workers, and named Woman of the Year by *Arkansas Democrat* readers.

1992    Became America's first lady after William J. Clinton is elected president of the United States.

1993    Began overseeing national task force dedicated to health-care reform.

1995    Became the first first lady to speak in China, where she hosted the Fourth World Conference on Women.

1996    Wrote *It Takes A Village*, for which she later received a spoken-word Grammy.

1997    Hosts conference on child care in Kansas City.

# INDEX

# PICTURE CREDITS

**Richard Kozar** is a former newspaper publisher and writer in Western Pennsylvania. He and his wife, Heidi, have two children, Caty and Macy.

**Matina S. Horner** is president emerita of Radcliffe College and associate professor of psychology and social relations at Harvard University. She is best known for her studies of women's motivation, achievement, and personality development. Dr. Horner has served on several national boards and advisory councils, including those of the National Science Foundation, Time Inc., and the Women's Research and Education Institute. She earned her B.A. from Bryn Mawr College and Ph.D. from the University of Michigan, and holds honorary degrees from many colleges and universities, including Mount Holyoke, Smith, Tufts, and the University of Pennsylvania.